Messages From My Grandparents... In Heaven

How You Can Keep Contact With Yours

ANDREA R. FREEMAN

BALBOA.
PRESS

A DIVISION OF HAY HOUSE

Balboa Press books may be ordered through booksellers or by contacting:

Balboa Press
A Division of Hay House
1663 Liberty Drive
Bloomington, IN 47403
www.balboapress.com
1 (877) 407-4847

Because of the dynamic nature of the Internet, any web addresses or links contained in this book may have changed since publication and may no longer be valid. The views expressed in this work are solely those of the author and do not necessarily reflect the views of the publisher, and the publisher hereby disclaims any responsibility for them.

The author of this book does not dispense medical advice or prescribe the use of any technique as a form of treatment for physical, emotional, or medical problems without the advice of a physician, either directly or indirectly. The intent of the author is only to offer information of a general nature to help you in your quest for emotional and spiritual well-being. In the event you use any of the information in this book for yourself, which is your constitutional right, the author and the publisher assume no responsibility for your actions.

Any people depicted in stock imagery provided by Thinkstock are models, and such images are being used for illustrative purposes only.
Certain stock imagery © Thinkstock.

Print information available on the last page.

ISBN: 978-1-5043-4986-4 (sc)
ISBN: 978-1-5043-4987-1 (hc)
ISBN: 978-1-5043-4988-8 (e)

Library of Congress Control Number: 2016901440

Balboa Press rev. date: 3/11/2016

Metaphysical methods listed in this book are for entertainment purposes only and are not intended for diagnosis or treatment of any condition. Please see a licensed doctor, psychiatrist, or counselor for diagnosis and treatment.

The material in this book reflects the intent of the author to offer advice/guidance toward your healing. If you wish to use the information in this book, it is your choice by right, and the author is not responsible for your action to do so.

The experiences stated in this book are valid; however, some names and details have been modified to protect the identities of those mentioned.

To my husband, family, friends, clients, and my dear readers: When we remember to look from within, those who have passed on never really left us.

ACKNOWLEDGMENTS

I am forever grateful to God, Jesus, my guardian angels and archangels for enabling me to share their comforting messages and my gifts to all. You motivated me to write this book—with and for my grandparents.

I send an everlasting thank-you to my grandparents for their constant love, strength, and guidance—once on earth and now in heaven—and for my family. I wouldn't be here without them.

Tremendous thank you to my loving parents, Sandy and John, who assisted me in rediscovering my grandparents' lives; provided me with an education, a roof over my head, and love in their hearts and for raising me well in a sometimes unstable world. I appreciate all that you still do.

Thank you to my beautiful sister Jana and cousin Angel -- her precious buglings, my wonderful in-laws, Nina and Don, my handsome and hilarious brothers, John and Andrew, my sweet cousin Alissa, my entire family, and all of my incredible friends, especially Jessica, Deanna, Mary, Erica, Hana, Claudia, Shari, Doreen, Cindy, Allen, and "Table 10" for constantly encouraging me while I discovered and shared my gifts and composed this book.

Enormous thanks to Danelle from the Beach Walk Hotel in Ocean City, Maryland; my wonderful clients, especially from my angel reading parties; and followers on Facebook, Twitter and Instagram for connecting with me and for their kind support and love of angels.

I am very grateful for the teachings/writings of Louise L. Hay, Doreen Virtue, Radleigh Valentine, Charles Virtue, Melissa Virtue, Jerry and Esther Hicks, James Van Praagh, Michael Newton, Christine Richardson, Dr. Wayne Dyer and other metaphysical writers. They have taught me so much and helped open my eyes to "remember who I am."

I am blessed to have discovered Balboa Press and its ability to bring my story and the stories of so many other writers to print. Thank you

Jade, Walter, the editors and the design team for your time and patience during the publishing process.

For those who have purchased this book, thank you so much for your interest and your willingness to heal your life.

Thanks ever so much to Joseph Bartolotta for visually bringing my book to life with such enchanting, lifelike artwork that captures the soul. You truly are incredibly gifted!

And to my compassionate, optimistic, loving husband and best friend, Anthony, thank you for standing by my side and strengthening me to follow my dream to write. Your gentle eyes and soul never wavered in keeping me focused during this incredible journey. I love you with all my heart!

CONTENTS

Introduction

Embracing Your Willingness to Communicate

I was not yet on this earth when my father's mother departed. I was four years old when my grandfather on my father's side passed away. When I was a year away from getting married at thirty-two, my grandmother on my mother's side went back home to heaven. Despite these age differences, I've learned and experienced through the years that all three of my grandparents have impacted my life in various ways while on earth and now in heaven. Even my grandmother, whom I never met still connects with me today. They are all truly my guardian angels.

The passing of a loved one is never easy. There can be so many words left unsaid or plans still not arranged. It sometimes happens suddenly—or it's just a matter of days. Among the many types of relationships that are hardest to face, losing a grandparent can be agonizing. They are the grounding, the bedrock of your family. Your idols suddenly aren't physically there anymore. Your grandparents may have even raised you if your biological parents were deceased. This could make a grandparent's passing even more difficult. No matter what role your grandparents have played in your life, their connection doesn't end when they leave this earth.

As a Certified Angel Card Reader, Angelic Life Coach, and someone who has studied metaphysics, I've come to know that my grandparents' spirits never left and their love never wavered. I strongly feel their presence in many ways, through my clairvoyant (clear seeing) and clairsentient (clear feeling) abilities. (These abilities are explained further in chapter I.) My visions and intuitiveness have ensured me that my grandparents are now healthier and happier. Surrounded by harmony, they watch vigilantly over me.

Whether or not you are aware of these abilities, you can still feel a connection with your grandparents. Our deceased loved ones leave numerous signs for us to recognize. In this book, you will discover how to identify these signs and possibly discover some of your own. Your experiences may mirror the ones I have encountered. Your life experiences don't matter; you just have to be open to the messages given by those you have lost and be clear to receive them.

The grief can be grim and deep; without knowing it, you may block yourself from receiving messages from your grandparents or other loved ones. It may feel like it's taking forever to receive the connection or a sign that you need. As you read this book, you'll discover that some—or all—of these reasons may pertain to you or someone you know who is facing the loss of a grandparent.

Everyone Grieves Differently

There's no specific way to grieve for the loss of a grandparent or a loved one. We all try to handle this deep emotion in the best way we can when it arrives. There are many stages and steps in individual healing. Some stay quiet and wish to be alone. Others prefer to be around many people and reminisce about those they lost. There are even those who ask, *Why haven't I cried yet? Is there something wrong with me?* I faced similar questions in 2011.

When I was growing up, I attended various wakes—but not funerals due to my age then. There were passing's of neighbors, friends of the family, or family members I had never met or only knew vaguely. I remember feeling sad, but I didn't understand the depth of what it meant to lose someone. At one wake, I watched a dear neighbor as she looked upon her husband who had passed. I sensed what she might have been feeling, but I did not fully feel the hurt.

When my grandfather died, I was only four. I don't remember crying when I heard of his passing. While composing this book, I asked my father, *"What did you tell me when I was younger about why Papa wasn't alive anymore?"*

My father had explained, *"Papa is with God and Jesus in heaven now."* My younger self took the news well. I was comforted because I knew a place was waiting and ready for my grandfather. Something inside me knew that death wasn't an ending. Children see the hope and the real truth behind what life truly embodies.

When my Grandma Marie passed away in 2011, I finally was greeted with my first multilevel impact of loss as an adult. It started with a call early in the morning from my mother Sandy. When she started to speak, I knew something was wrong. I had known my grandmother was sick and had few remaining options, but I was still shocked when I finally received word.

I cried, *"I was supposed to see her, and I didn't last week. Oh God, Noooo!!!! I was supposed to see her!"*

I had prayed to her soul and to her angels while she was sick. If she needed to go and wanted to release herself from the pain, she had to do what she needed to do. I had prayed that I would still love and understand her and could release her so she could find peace. About two weeks later, she passed tranquilly in her sleep.

I didn't cry heavily during the wake; I just gazed at how beautiful she looked during her viewing. On one night between the wakes, I had my first visit with my grandma. I felt her leaning over me and hugging my right side as I was trying to fall asleep. Through my cognizant (clear knowing) abilities, I knew I'd see her again one day. I instantly knew she wasn't far away despite her physically not being here on earth. I understood she was where she needed to be. A knowingness washed over me. Just like I'm sure that one plus one equals two, I had an unwavering notion of her essence.

After her funeral, the afternoon sun confidently broke through the vast cumulus lineup. I recognized her soul was smiling through the March sky. That warm, peaceful, encouraging moment made me smile instantaneously. The sun definitely had more gleam than usual; Grandma revealed to us all that she was in no more discomfort.

Some months later, I visited my parents' house in Brooklyn. On the way, I felt a need to pass by my grandmother's old apartment. She had lived about fifteen minutes away from my parents. I stepped outside my fiancé's (at the time) double-parked car and walked toward my healing. I walked through the last few layers of experiencing the loss of Grandma Marie.

I hadn't been near the front door of her apartment complex in so long. Everything looked the same: the angle of the walkway, the four garbage pails on the left side, and the gray chains swooping in front of them. The golden light still shined downward, revealing the doorway, the call box, and her red-brown brick building.

I hovered my finger over 2C and pressed it in my mind to gain entrance. I heard the entry door buzzing loudly and clearly. My body remained standing there, but my memories led me inside as the door opened with a familiar heavy click inside my mind.

***

As always, the hallway was nicely heated and I felt safe when I entered. Sometimes Grandma Marie would call my name as I walked up the stairs. She always worried about my safety—even at an older age. Her protective words of wisdom—*"Don't talk to strangers!"* and *"Don't take candy from strangers!"*—were recited during each visit.

On the second landing, I turned the corner in my mind's eye. I saw her waiting by the door. She was so tiny and cute in her cozy, warm, sweat outfit. The loving glow of her interior lights always cast a welcoming aura around her. That hue always let me know the love of a grandmother is forever. If I stood in that memory more, I could relive each joyous moment in her apartment by the water, the many meals she cooked for me, and her stories about growing up.

I walked back to the car, and the floodgates opened. I finally had the cry that had taken so long to show itself. My fiancé held me tightly and let me spill out every last ounce of tears that I knew needed to be released.

I sobbed, *"I just want to go up there and really see her!"*

After letting out my last tears, my fiancé and I drove away from my grandmother's old block. I looked to the window where she always waved and watched for visitors. The tenant who had moved in after her no longer resided there. It was the only floor with no occupants or curtains. With all the lights off, I could see her waving to me.

***

When there are so many people at a wake or funeral, you sometimes don't have time to cry. If you are wrapped up in the formalities of the day's events and occupied with loving family and friends, you might want to focus on the good memories.

However, when those tears finally come, it's okay because they come when you need them the most. There isn't anything wrong with you; it is part of your healing. Even when you know your loved one is in a better place, its okay to release those tears—even long after someone has passed. Everyone grieves differently and at different times. When you are ready to reach for the next positive thought, you will notice a change in your emotions. You can let go of the pain and make room for the cleansing within.

Moving on from the loss of a grandparent or other loved one is easier said than done. You may feel numb or at a loss for time. You may question whether your reality without that person actually happened. Your goals can include mending bridges for inner peace and filling the void with love. It all takes time, and you needn't be hard on yourself during this process. You are never alone, because God, your angels, and others will definitely make sure you move forward little by little with the grace of unconditional love.

My Prayers for You …

I felt compelled to write this book because I sensed a connection with my grandparents. Many people have lost grandparents and miss that special love that only they can deliver. This book is not limited to healing the loss of grandparents. This information can help mend your heart after the loss of other beautiful and incredible individuals. It can be agonizing to move forward from a loss when all you want to do is hear a familiar voice, hold a comforting hand, or feel a warm embrace.

This book will help you get through the time until next you meet your loved ones. Where there is love and faith, miracles will follow with patience and trust.

From personal experiences and metaphysical studies, I know your grandparents/loved ones still keep contact. After reading this book, you'll be able to identify the signs in your daily life and understand why they come about. I also offer ways to keep in contact with my grandparents.

I pray that you can courageously take a journey with me, rediscover the connection that still breathes life between you and your grandparents, willingly embrace your abilities, and never feel distant from them. You will finally feel comfortable and confirm that you're not imagining whatever communication experiences you have had.

I want to thank you for choosing this book. On the pages that follow, allow yourself to embark on a course toward restoring clarity and balance in your life. I thank you in advance for keeping an open mind about any metaphysical terms you are unfamiliar with. You can take any topics that interest you and incorporate them into your life. Choose the ones you feel most comfortable with. There is no pressure to agree with all the terminology in this book, and it doesn't matter what religion you follow. Angels provide guidance to anyone who wants to receive daily messages.

God, your guardian angels, and your grandparents are with you each and every step you take. They are always patient and ready. As you begin your days of healing, I wish you blessed guidance, inspiration, and comfort!

CHAPTER I

See, Hear, Feel, Know

Perhaps they are not stars, but rather openings in heaven where the love of our lost ones pours through and shines down upon us to let us know they are happy.

—Eskimo proverb

You might be feeling too much grief, guilt, or sadness to feel your grandparents' presence. There might be things you didn't get to do with or for your loved ones before their passing. Human emotions on earth are nonexistent in heaven. There is no sadness, pain, anger, guilt, or fear there. There is only unconditional love, happiness, and peace. Living in the present moment—and not dwelling on the past—is real to those now in heaven. They do not look down upon us with disgust. There is a journey that we all must fulfill, and we can only try our best to live it. Those who have left this earth before us only wish to encourage us, and they would never feel shame or disappointment if we failed at something.

Once you're ready and willing to understand this and you release yourself from feeling any guilt due to your loved one's passing, you can begin to lift away the barrier you have put up against communicating with your grandparents or other loved ones. You will start to find your inner peace again and connect better with your higher self—the spiritual part of you that is connected to the wisdom of heaven.

You may not feel the presence of those who have passed on, because you are not open to various ways of communicating with them. In metaphysical studies (a branch of philosophy that explains the fundamental nature of reality as *being* and the *world* that encompasses it), there are four Clairs. They represent the abilities to connect through vision (clairvoyance), hearing (clairaudience), feeling (clairsentience), and knowing (claircognizance).

These communication methods or channels help us receive guidance and messages from God, our guardian angels, and loved ones who have passed. If you're having difficulty receiving messages, these areas might be blocked—and those ways of communicating will not be receptive. They may be closed because you aren't aware of their functions, or something may have occurred in your life that caused these intuitive abilities to be clouded.

Everyone has the capability to receive messages and guidance through these four channels. We all have at least one or two communication abilities that are naturally open. The others, through time, can also be developed further if you wish.

For each Clair description, I add my personal accounts with them. You might find a correlation to what you have already experienced that perhaps you didn't realize connects with these communication channels.

Clairvoyance (Clear Seeing)

This natural, intuitive guidance comes through visions that you see inside or outside your mind. These visions are recognized as small scenes within your mind's eye or images you see before you. If you see a coin or a feather on the ground, a heart-shaped cloud formation, or a rainbow after praying for your loved one, you are receiving direct visual messages from them.

In your mind's eye—or your third eye—you might see visions of situations and certain people within them. You may also notice that what you're seeing always arrives at the precise moment you need an answer.

It's quite possible that you can receive visual messages/images in your dream state. If you recently dreamed of a favorite blanket your grandmother made for you, you may have been thinking about her during your waking hours prior to the dream.

If you notice that, as a whole, you connect more with visual things in your daily life, then this Clair might be one of your natural communication abilities. However, if you dismiss these visual signs and feel you are imagining them, this communication ability may not function strongly. When you doubt what you see, you're closing and narrowing the window of opportunity that could make this ability grow stronger for you.

One of my natural communication abilities comes through as clairvoyance, especially while I conduct angel readings. Angel readings connect you with your guardian angels. They lovingly give you messages of guidance and advice in all areas of your life. I use specific angel card decks to do this. (More information on angel readings can be found in Chapter III.)

During one of my angel reading sessions for a client, I was able to see with my mind's eye the Blessed Mother Mary relay a message for me and for my client, Jessica. I was able to see Mother Mary lean over my right shoulder and rest her right hand upon it. The visual was like a mother looking over her child's shoulder when the child is doing homework. This image had a caring, vigilant, loving, and engaging appearance to it. I knew Mother Mary wanted me to tell Jessica that she was connected with her and was lovingly guiding her daily. I had no prior knowledge of Jessica's connection with Mother Mary, but after our angel reading session, Jessica mentioned how she would often pray to the statue of the Blessed Mother Mary when she passed the church in her neighborhood.

Your angels can visually relay messages through various ranges of light. For example, have you ever noticed various colors of little sparkles of light around you during the day or night? If so, these glittering, sparkling specks of light are the aura colors of your archangels or angels. Auras can identify which archangel or angel is with you since each one has a different color and representation of its abilities.

To briefly explain, while conducting angel readings, I often work closely with four out of the many archangels that are around us. The chart "Archangel Guidance" lists these four archangels, their representing colors, and how they assist us daily. While talking to the client, I would see these archangels' auras sparkle, as listed in the chart, along with sometimes silver light. I also see these lights when casually out with friends. Most of the time—if I'm out in nature—I see golden sparkles of light. Seeing these glimmering lights lets me know my angels are guiding me or informing me that they are with those I'm spending time with.

Archangel Guidance

Archangel	Color	Ability/ Helps With/ Provides
Michael	royal purple, royal blue, sometimes gold	protection, courage, security, confidence
Raphael	emerald green	healing, travel, guidance for healers
Jophiel	different shades of pink	beauty, grace of the inner heart, clears and organizes
Gabriel	copper, sometimes gold	communication, creativity, helps those who are messengers, protects children

So right about now, you're probably thinking, *Seeing all these flashes of light, perhaps you should consider going for an eye exam to find out if there's something wrong with your eyesight.* This is a perfectly normal reaction. Rest assured, I've gone for regular checkups, and all is perfectly well with my vision. These sparkles of light are just a colorful and creative way for your angels to connect with you visually. If you are open to it, you will notice it quite often. Please take caution though. If you notice something troubling your eyesight that goes beyond the realm of what I've mentioned here, don't ignore those signs. Please see an eye doctor to diagnose treatment.

Auras

Humans also have auras. The color fields that surround our bodies represent our energy, which can be seen by clairvoyants. Aura colors range from different tones and shades that can change based on your mood, what you are accomplishing or experiencing in life, and other people's impact on you. You may have the ability to see the auras of other individuals. Have you ever noticed a pink glow around people while talking to them?

When I was a young adolescent, I was sitting in my cousin's car. I saw golden light emanating out from her and around her. I was too young to realize that I was witnessing her aura, which reflected her high spiritual vibration and integrity. I felt a comforting, safe, loving presence from the light. I had been going through some tough times, and seeing that light was a confirmation that all was well. I knew she would be there to protect me.

The following chart lists the various aura colors that you might see. It includes the representation that your guardian angels want you to be aware of. In the "Aura Meaning" section, you will notice color descriptions and color contrasts that will reflect whether the auras are shining vibrantly. If they need healing work, they will reflect darker, cloudier colors.

Aura Color	Aura Meaning
Red	Determination/Frustration
Orange	Creativity/Lacking Reason
Yellow	Happiness/Ego-Driven
Green	Nurturing/Jealousy
Blue	Freethinking/Sadness

Purple	Intuition/Authoritative
Brown	Grounding/Feeling Worthless
Black	Lack of Forgiveness/Hatred
Pink	Self-Love/Tenderness
White (Cloudy)	Denial/Cover-Up
White (Clear)	Compassionate/Inspiration
Gold	Integrity/Clear-seeing/High Spiritual Vibration

Clairaudience (Clear Hearing)

This natural intuitive guidance comes through what you hear from either outside or inside your mind. Sounds outside your mind can pertain to various things that you may not have realized hold deep meanings for you.

For instance, when was the last time you listened to a song repetitively? Was it something about the melody? Did you like the catchy chorus? Did it remind you of someone else? Did it answer your questions? What time of the day was it? All of these questions hold the key to why your angels or grandparents/loved ones are trying to send you messages through auditory means.

Another client had a similar encounter with messages through songs. Mary's husband had passed, and she was worried about some matters in her life. Right after praying and thinking about her husband and surrendering and releasing her concerns, her wedding song played on the car radio. Mary knew automatically that her husband was contacting her to let her know that all would be well—and that he would see her through every aspect of her life with strength.

The next time you listen to music, take notice of the following:

- ❖ What genre is it?
- ❖ What time of day did you hear it?
- ❖ How many times have you replayed it?

❖ What were you thinking of prior to it?
❖ Which lyrics/melodies grab your attention?

Songs are a playful and encouraging way for your angels and grandparents/loved ones who have passed to get your attention.

Another way your angels try to get your attention through hearing is when divine timing allows you to be at the right place at the right time and you overhear a conversation that might benefit your situation. If you are shopping or traveling to work on a bus or train, you might overhear a conversation where someone is in a similar situation. The person may say something profound that signals you to know how to tackle your current situation. This is your angel's way of helping you through your daily life.

You can also receive messages from inside your mind. This internal voice may sound like your voice or like someone else's voice. Don't let this scare you. I'm not talking about horror movies that scare you at night.

When I was in my twenties, I was running errands in my neighborhood. I was driving around alone and reflecting upon a discussion I'd had with someone earlier that day. I was confused and unsettled. While I was trying to understand why the dialogue took place, I heard a voice say, *"She has fears."* There was definitely no one in the car with me, and I didn't have the radio on. It was a calm, still, male voice that I didn't recognize at first. However, after I assessed the situation further, I realized it was Archangel Michael giving me a guided message to help me feel more secure about the situation.

When I was around eight, I was ordering takeout food with my parents. Out of nowhere, I was able to hear my cousin saying my name. My parents and I had just visited her, and we lived an hour and a half away from each other. I clearly was nowhere near her, but I was still able to hear her voice. She also has these abilities. When I spoke to her on the phone about this occurrence, she revealed that she was saying my name quietly to herself because she missed me. It still amazes me that I was able to hear her!

I can still hear high-pitched sounds with shifting pressure from each ear. This sensation doesn't bring any discomfort to me at all. I know my angels are trying to send me messages. Their vibrations are higher and faster than ours, and we tend to hear them as high-pitched sounds. The noises resemble an old television set being turned on in the other room. You can feel the elevated difference in sound—closer to you and switching between your ears. If you have experienced this, ask your angels to speak slower and lower to you so you can better understand their messages. You may notice a revelation or an answer to a question popping up soon after hearing the sound. Again, take caution. If you discover pain, discomfort, or ringing in your ears beyond the scope of what is mentioned here, don't ignore the signs. Please see a doctor who can diagnose treatment.

If you pay close attention to people's voices and music every day, clairaudience is one of your natural communication abilities.

Clairsentience, (Clear Feeling)

This natural intuitive guidance involves receiving messages through your five senses and also through emotional or physical sensations. This is my second most natural communication ability.

Messages through the Sense of Smell

When I was living with my parents, I would smell my father's cologne a couple of hours before he would come home from work. I feel that this was my angel's way—and possibly my grandfather's way—of letting me know that my father was safe and would be home soon. I would sometimes smell incense or candles without any of them burning near me. When this would occur, I felt that it was my guardian angels connecting with me and delivering a message of pure inner peace.

Messages through the Sense of Touch

Walking in the park is one of my favorite pastimes. I recall one beautiful, humidity-free day in Staten Island, New York, the sweet summer air felt cool and gentle. It was warm enough that I didn't need a jacket. While I was reviewing some situations that were troubling me, I felt a warm embrace from within my heart. It expanded all over my body. It felt as if someone was hugging me, yet I was not walking with anyone. I smiled and felt reassured that my angels and my grandfather were comforting me.

Messages through the Sense of Hearing

During another reading with Mary, I was able to feel and hear the demeanor of her late husband. I didn't know her husband very well prior to his passing, but I was able to confirm his messages for Mary through my clairsentience and clairaudience. I used Doreen Virtue and James Van Praagh's *Talking to Heaven Mediumship Cards,* and one of the cards validated his beautiful message for Mary: *Life is a series of choices. Choose love.*

Mary knew it was her husband's way of seeing life.

Messages through the Sense of Sight

Whenever I read for Deanna, her feelings about her father who passed always come through. It doesn't matter what topic is being discussed; he always wants his presence known. One of the ways he does this is through his lighthearted humor. As I bless/meditate on the cards in front of Deanna, a random card—or cards—will always flip out of the deck, causing fumbling of the other cards. It's something I only notice when reading for Deanna. We both laugh since we know he is joking with us and bringing some fun into the reading.

Messages through Emotional Sensations

At the end of October 2013, my husband and I took a cruise to the Caribbean. As we were walking the promenade deck one night, my clairsentience really kicked in!

Dressed in our captain's night finest, we passed several photo screen options for our evening pictures. Immersed in all the heightened glitz and glamour, I felt something catch my attention besides the wondrous festivities surrounding us. I felt a strong, heavy, familiar presence within my chest. It was definitely not a heart attack; it wasn't painful or uncomfortable. I knew the deep pulling of my attention was recognizable; a dear friend of mine who passed away days before my wedding in September 2012.

Ron brought great laughter into my late teens and my early twenties. He reintroduced me to the eighties through screenplays and lyrics. He taught me how to shoot pool, and he could make an outstanding cappuccino. When I found out that Ron had died, I felt so guilty for not keeping in touch with him more. I conversed mostly via text with him, especially my last text to confirm that he would be able to attend my wedding. Since his passing, I've come to terms with it being okay that we didn't connect as much later on in life. I realized Ron was busy in his own way. Though I miss him very much, I know we can keep in contact on a different level.

The sudden connection I felt toward Ron on the cruise ship was linked to a photo screen of the famous Titanic's main stairway. When James Cameron's 1997 blockbuster movie *Titanic* premiered, Ron and I watched it two or three times in the movie theater. We loved its haunting theme song.

Whenever I see/hear anything associated with Titanic, I feel Ron's presence so prominently. A particular instance that still gives me goosebumps was on the day of his birthday. I felt compelled to post a heartfelt message to Ron on his Facebook page even though I knew he wasn't physically on this earth anymore. After a few hours of posting my message, I had to step out and add money unto my metro card. I tried to use one of the machines in Grand Central Terminal, but it malfunctioned. I then proceeded to walk toward the opposite section of the terminal to use another machine. As I descended the stairs, I heard a well-known song. Street performs were playing their rendition of Celine Dion's *My Heart Will Go On,* which was one of the music tracks for the movie *Titanic* and the song Ron and I loved so much. The odds of that song playing in the terminal were extremely low. However, there are no coincidences and everything definitely happens for a reason. I was meant to use the other machine that day, even though the original machine I attempted to use usually works. Hearing the song was a strong confirmation/message from Ron, acknowledging and thanking me for remembering him on his birthday.

If you receive emotional sensations from those who have passed, each sensation will seem different because it pertains to the person who is connecting with you. It's almost like having a secret code that represents so much to you and your loved one.

With clairsentience, you can also sense the character of people before you get to really know them. I am able to sense the character of others by feeling their energy, and I know where their true intentions dwell. You can probably sense this too, and you shouldn't dismiss it when it arises. When you feel intuition, a gut feeling, or a hunch kicking in, your angels are guiding and protecting you. If you discover that you are sensitive to emotions around you, this is your natural communication style.

Claircognizance (Clear Knowing)

This natural intuitive guidance involves knowing information without prior knowledge. This can come through as predictions, premonitions, dreams, or déjà vu. The time frames of your clear knowing can include past, present, and future.

As a Claircognizant, you might discover that you quite often finish other people's sentences before they do. This is not a coincidence; it is the ability to connect and mentally download the enlightened messages from your angels.

Déjà vu can be related to past lives and reincarnation. Past lives are where an individual has lived through many lifetimes, countries, cultures, generations, and time frames. Reincarnation is a rebirth of the soul that lives through these various lifetimes, coming back as different genders and/or professions.

For example if you decide to take a dance class, and the instructor demonstrates new moves, you pick up on the instructions immediately. Your movements are effortless, and you flow gracefully—without prior dance instruction. This might suggest that you were a dancer in a past life. You carry the knowledge, talents, and abilities from past reincarnations into your current life.

I've encountered moments where I felt I had prior knowledge to something without any proof. For another client, I felt strongly that she had been a barmaid in the 1880s. I couldn't tell exactly why I knew it, but I was confident. I could see an image of her barmaid uniform over her regular clothes.

If you surround yourself with messages and meanings and have deep knowledge on various topics or activities without any prior knowledge, this could be your natural communication ability. To fully know which Clair matches you best, angel readings can determine a precise link.

CHAPTER II

A Chakra a Day Keeps the Negativity Away

In metaphysical studies, chakras (pronounced Shock-ruhs), are one of the major ways to help you understand and maintain your inner balance. Chakras are invisible energy centers/auras within and around your body, which are influenced by your daily thoughts. Your thoughts control the energy flow within your chakras. The higher the vibration of your thoughts, the more connected you are to feeling open and receptive to the good around you. The higher the vibration of each chakra, the more vibrant the auras/colors of each chakra will appear.

You have many chakras, but eight are most commonly known. They spin like wheels—and look like invisible fan blades—of color auras. These are known as the root, sacral, solar, heart, throat, ear, third eye, and crown chakras. (Please refer to "Placement of Your Chakras" on the back cover to locate your chakras and their associated colors.) The lower chakras—starting at the root—pertain to materialistic thoughts and beliefs. The upper chakras, starting with the heart, are your spiritual thoughts and beliefs.

In this book, I will only discuss the four chakras (heart, third-eye, ear, and crown chakras) that are linked to the four Clairs. These four chakras relate to your thoughts/beliefs/actions in spiritual matters. If these four chakras are blocked, you won't be able to connect with your Clairs. If these four chakras are open, you are receptive to guidance from God, your angels, and your loved ones whom have passed. When you are open to guidance and become more accustomed to focusing on the significance of each chakra, less negativity resides within you.

Heart Chakra

Your clairsentience is associated with your heart chakra. This spinning chakra is green and is located at the center of your chest. The heart chakra represents thoughts/beliefs/actions you have about the following:

- ❖ how you handle your emotions
- ❖ how you can forgive yourself and others
- ❖ how comfortable you are with receiving and giving love
- ❖ your thoughts surrounding love
- ❖ how willing you are to let yourself heal and let go of the past and experiences/emotions that have troubled you

Third-Eye Chakra

Your clairvoyance is associated with the third-eye chakra. This indigo chakra is located between your two physical eyes. The third-eye chakra represents thoughts/beliefs/actions you have about the following:

- ❖ how comfortable you are receiving guidance from god and your angels through your intuitiveness, insights, and visions
- ❖ how comfortable you are doing manifesting and visualization work toward your future goals.

Ear Chakra

Your clairaudience is associated with your ear chakra. This red-violet chakra is located inside your head, above your ears. This represents thoughts/beliefs/actions you have about the following:

- ❖ how comfortable you are with hearing guidance from God and your angels
- ❖ how you can emotionally handle hearing what is said about you

Crown Chakra

Your claircognizance is associated with your crown chakra. This purple chakra spins at the highest vibration of all the chakras, and it is located inside the top of your head. The crown chakra represents thoughts/beliefs/actions you have about the following:

❖ Spirituality and how you connect with its knowingness (intuitive messages)
❖ Enlightenment/wisdom you receive from God and your angels

Whatever you think about daily—and the duration and frequency within each thought—determines how you feel and what you will experience in your life, affecting your chakras and sometimes your health. If you are blocked in one of these areas, it may mean you are either thinking too negatively regarding specific thoughts represented by the chakras or tragic experiences in certain areas of your life pertain to that chakra.

Your chakras will be affected, and they need to be cleared out. This is not cause for alarm; it is just a way to know what needs to be balanced in your life. You'll notice if you feel drained, tired, or irritable. If you have physical ailments or chronic pain, you may need to improve. It's all about how you perceive matters in life and choosing to have a brighter outlook toward what you experience. You can't control what happens in life, but you can control how you react.

You can learn more about the care of your chakras and if they need to be healed in the following ways:

❖ See a licensed Reiki practitioner (hands-on healer who exchanges healing energy while hovering over chakras of a clothed patient)
❖ Have an angel card reading to connect with your guardian angels. This will reveal information about your chakras and other guidance/messages (through the cards provided).
❖ Practice daily meditation, visualization, and affirmation work for each chakra in your own home.

❖ Work with crystals that have healing properties pertaining to each chakra.

❖ Change to a healthier diet. Certain food and beverages have energy that can block your chakras and not make them as clear and receptive.

❖ Exercise more. Focus on cardio, core-strength workouts, yoga, and pilates if possible.

❖ Flower Healing (naturopath studies show the benefits through healing properties of various species of flowers)

CHAPTER III

Being Patient through the Transitioning Period

Learning about your Clairs and chakras might seem a bit overwhelming at first. You are embracing different parts of yourself that you didn't know existed or didn't realize you were already experiencing. The connection of your physical self and your spiritual or higher self (intuitiveness) is reawakening. Take the time to familiarize yourself with each area—and feel free to reread the first two chapters as much as you need to. There's no rush, and it's quite beneficial to really know what your abilities are, which can enhance your connection with your loved ones.

After taking the necessary time to channel your abilities and open your Clairs and chakras, you may find yourself still saying, "Why haven't I made a connection with my loved one?" or "I know what to look for, but why can't I see, hear, or feel them?" The transitioning process involves those who are trying to heal from loss and also those who have left earth. Those departed must indeed go through their own transition periods.

Your healing encompasses the ability to break free from misunderstood perceptions and assumptions that may swirl in your mind when someone you love has passed away. Your loved ones need the same respect, time, and patience in heaven.

Your Healing Process

To understand the transition period further, let's look at it from two perspectives. First from your own healing progression:

There is no set timetable. There is not a one-size-fits-all healing strategy that is required. Depending on the type of loss you have experienced, there are many variations to recovery. It is all based upon the individual. Patience with yourself is key. True healing can only be beneficial if you are truly willing and ready to take the necessary steps forward, if you are surrounded by those who care and support you through your time of need, and if you are ready to quiet your mind and allow yourself to believe you can connect with those who have passed. Optimism is also key.

As discussed in previous chapters, guilt, anger, and regret can block you from feeling the love and guidance you're expecting to feel from your loved one. Sometimes you have to allow yourself to feel these emotions in order to move forward. Stuffing down your true feelings or not acknowledging them at all can also delay your healing. It is common, normal, and understandable to feel many emotions when a loved one passes. The trick is knowing when and why you have to move toward more positive realizations.

Common emotions and ways of thinking that occur after the loss of a loved one include the following:

- ❖ *Overwhelmed*: There is so much to plan, think about, and focus on. Life continues—and so do your responsibilities.
- ❖ *Shock/Denial*: It still doesn't feel real. You're taken by surprise. It just can't be true. You may be taking care of everyone else—and be denying healing for yourself.
- ❖ *Numbness/Depression*: You feel as if the happiness has been stolen from you. Where there once was vitality, there is predictable hollowness.
- ❖ *Loneliness*: You have lost all you had in your life. You might think no one can understand what you're feeling.
- ❖ *Guilt/Regret*: You may feel that you didn't do enough to help your loved one, that you should have made other choices to help, or that you should have spent more time with your loved one. You may regret knowing your loved one and the time you had with him or her, because you feel your time together is now over.

❖ *Doubt/Discouragement*: Your loss has made you question if there is a God that could allow this loss. You feel less positive in the joys that life could bring and can't look forward to anything new.

❖ *Anger*: You are mad at your loved one because he or she was careless in life. You're infuriated with your loved one for not reaching out to you sooner. You're angry with yourself for not noticing the signs that he or she was in need. You're enraged with the hospital and doctors because you feel they overlooked or mistreated your loved one. You ignore God because you feel he has taken your loved one away from you too soon.

Which Way To Go?

These emotions can also be found on the Emotional Guidance System Scale. Esther Hicks, motivational, metaphysical speaker and author, has mentioned that we all have an emotional guidance system. It's a scale of emotions that we experience every day. Think of this system as a GPS for humans. How you are feeling on the scale directs you toward what's going on at the present moment in your life. It's like receiving red flags of awareness for what you need to change in your life or confirming that you're on the right path.

Joy is the highest sensation on this emotional scale, and fear is the lowest sensitivity. You shouldn't think less of yourself if you are feeling the lower moods on this scale; it's a signal for you to find a better thought. This scale can help you get through the healing process when you lose a loved one. No matter where you are on this scale, your guardian angels want you to know that there's always a new day and another chance to feel better.

The Esther Hicks Emotional Guidance System

Various emotions are arranged in order from the highest-feeling thoughts to the lowest-feeling thoughts. This scale can be used as a tool to know where your emotions currently reside and what you should strive toward in moving up the scale.

1. joy/knowledge/empowerment/freedom/love/appreciation
2. passion
3. enthusiasm/eagerness/happiness
4. positive expectation/belief
5. optimism
6. hopefulness
7. contentment
8. boredom
9. pessimism
10. frustration/irritation/impatience
11. "overwhelment"
12. disappointment
13. doubt
14. worry
15. blame
16. discouragement
17. anger
18. revenge
19. hatred/rage
20. jealousy
21. insecurity/guilt/unworthiness
22. fear/grief/depression/despair/powerlessness

Steps toward Moving Up the Emotional Guidance System Scale

❖ Acknowledge which emotion(s) you are feeling.
❖ Identify why you are feeling this emotion. What has sparked you to feel the way you are feeling? Create a time line of when these emotions have triggered.
❖ Locate where this emotion(s) is on the scale and see what the next higher emotion is to strive toward feeling better.
❖ Pray to God, your angels, or whomever you desire to help you move forward toward the next highest emotion. Ask for guidance and to receive distinct, consistent, and familiar signs

that will help you know how to move forward—and the best people to interact with on your road to recovery.

❖ Start each morning by thinking of five things that you are thankful for. If you can't, even thinking of just one thankful element in your life is better than nothing. It's a start, and you can always add on more as the days go on. It's crucial to not count the mistakes, mishaps, or unfortunate circumstances in your life. You will only attract more of those situations instead of the happier occurrences you'd rather connect with. When you look for the blessings in your life, you will notice that you are surrounded more by happiness, which will elevate your mood.

❖ Positive books, sayings, or affirmations are a great way to remind yourself what your positive goals are, and they can help you start your day on a brighter note. Starting your day in a place of peace determines the rest of your day. It's all about reaching for the next highest feeling thought.

❖ If you need further support while reaching your highest happiness, seek assistance from family, friends, coworkers, a psychologist, or a Certified Angel Card Reader. They might help uncover layers of suppressed emotions you weren't aware of.

You Have the Power within You To Make Every Day Your Best!

Angel readings are inspiring and comforting, especially when your emotions seem sporadic after losing a loved one. If angel readings are new to you—or if you have debated experiencing one—the next few pages might help introduce you to its special gifts. It is an alternate way of proceeding through your transitioning process.

Angel readings clarify what you can't always see or realize because of the severity of your situation. The guidance, inspiration, and comfort provided during each reading from your guardian angels contribute toward your motivation to move upward on the emotional guidance system scale. Like advice from a trusted friend, your guardian angels will guide you toward understanding your past and present situations, inspire you to choose more uplifting thought patterns, and offer comfort as you embark on your journey toward clarity in life.

As a Certified Angel Card Reader and Angelic Life Coach, I'm able to use my clairvoyant and clairsentient abilities to help people connect with their guardian angels through various card decks that reveal specific, safe, loving messages and images. I've been conducting readings since 2005 for family, friends, clients, and myself. I'm honored and blessed to have been certified through Doreen Virtue's first angel reading certification class and also her son Charles Virtue's Angelic Life Coaching class. Both these opportunities have opened the doors of my communication further, strongly increased my abilities, and enabled me to aid others to find purpose and restore balance in their lives.

Life shouldn't be a struggle; it should flow effortlessly. This is a common message we receive from our guardian angels daily. There are times when outside influences prevent us from clearly seeing the path we need to take, especially when dealing with the loss of a loved one. Your angels want you to rediscover your inner peace and understand that you deserve to live your life to the fullest. With each angel reading, you will feel more centered, happier, and more confident. You will pursue your dreams and live a balanced, abundant life. You will realize that you do have the power within you to make every day your best!

Your angels want you to choose joy and see the joy in everything you do. We all know this can be challenging. We are all human, and the angels are not claiming that we all will never feel livid or heartbroken again. However, your guardian angels want you to develop a way to bounce back quicker from bad days. Instead of being angry for three days, maybe you'll start to be mad for just one day and a half. We practice seeing joy in everything by being thankful for everything and everyone in our lives.

Your guardian angels watch over you, especially during this healing process. They know it takes time to heal. However, their loving goal for you is to move forward and try to feel a little better each day by reaching and choosing higher, more positive thoughts about yourself than you had the day before. Taking these small steps will move you in the direction of healing.

Finding Purpose through it All

I believe we will see all those we have interacted with on earth again in heaven. I believe we all have a purpose on earth and a reason for coming here. Those we interact with are part of fulfilling our purposes—and we help others with theirs. Those we have lost had a purpose, and part of it was the timing in which they had to leave us. It's hard to understand this at times, but everything will reveal itself with divine timing. It will become clear soon, and we must trust that everything happens for a reason. Don't be hard on yourself during this time, because you are doing the best you can. You and your departed loved one need to heal.

Sometimes the way in which our loved ones have gone teaches us about ourselves and our reasons for living. While writing this book, the beloved actor and comedian Robin Williams passed away on August 11, 2014, by committing suicide. Suicide is a controversial topic. Some say taking one's life makes that individual a coward or an inadequate person. I feel that it is a disease. Robin Williams—and many others— tried to fight it, but he couldn't hold out any longer. His death helped us celebrate his life, which was full of accomplishments. His missions empower us to see the potential we can find in others as well as ourselves. His passing allows us to remove the veil from our eyes and finally see a different side of what we thought depression and suicide really entail.

In 1991, Robin Williams played Dr. Malcolm Sayer in *Awakenings*. He said, "The human spirit is more powerful than any drug, and that is what needs to be nourished with work, play, friendship, family. These are the things that matter."

Through Robin William's life, we learn more about how our lives are truly intertwined for the purpose of others and what life encompasses.

***

I'd like to share with you, a video I watched from ESPN.com embodying how our individual purposes are connected. The video showcases how everything happens for a reason, and there is always hope in finding a purpose through it all when a loved one passes.

Bravery, selflessness, and commitment sum up the acts performed by a twenty-four-year-old named Welles Remy Crowther, also known to many as the "Man in the Red Bandanna." Born in Nyack, New York, on May 17, 1977, Welles grew up in a very loving family. A connection to his father helped nurture his purpose. As a child, Welles noticed that his father kept a blue or a red bandanna in his right hip pocket. Welles's unique interest in this encouraged his father Jefferson to purchase a red one for Welles. Since the age of six, Welles would always carry it with him—even under his sports uniforms/helmet while playing lacrosse at Boston College.

At the age of sixteen, Welles joined his father as a junior fireman volunteer, and he became a junior member of the Empire Hook and Ladder Company. Even at such a young age, Welles was already recognized as a smart, concentrated person who had skills and truly loved to help others. In 1999, Welles graduated with honors along with a degree in economics. He moved to New York City and accepted a job as an equities trader. This opportunity with Sandler O'Neill and Partners brought him to the 104th floor of the South Tower at the World Trade Center.

It was a clear, illuminating morning on September 11, 2001. It started off like any another workday for so many, but twelve people wouldn't expect to be connected to Welles's life purpose and be saved from something so unimaginable.

At 8:46am, American Airlines Flight 11 flew into the North Tower. Evacuations were underway in the South Tower. Approximately two hundred people in the Sky Lobby on the seventy-eighth floor of the South Tower were waiting to leave the building.

At 9:02am, United Airlines Flight 175 hit the South Tower, and its wings cut a treacherous path from the seventy-eighth to the eighty-fourth floors. Ling Young was thrown, severely burned, and saw no way out. She heard a young man call out. He was carrying a woman on his back and notifying everyone he found in a stairwell to exit and follow him. He advised the surviving people around him to help those they could. Ling recounts that the way he said it—with his strong, authoritative voice—she just knew to follow him. Welles led Ling and others to the only functional stairway on the seventy-eighth floor and traveled fifteen floors down to the sixty-first floor. He left them in the care of firefighters who could lead the survivors to working elevators. Welles went back up the stairs to save more lives.

Climbing seventeen floors, Welles encountered Judy Wein. He put out fires and aided the wounded. Judy suffered a broken arm, cracked ribs, and a punctured lung. When Judy saw Welles, she remembers him announcing to those around him to stand and help others if they were capable. Welles went back to help anyone he could find in need. At 9:59am, the South Tower collapsed.

Six months later, on March 19, 2002, Welles's body, intact and not burned, was found in what could have been the remains of the lobby of the South Tower, near firemen who were also recovered. In May of that year, Welles's mother stumbled upon an article in the *New York Times* that issued accounts of those who survived the South Tower. One passage immediately called out to Allison. Judy Wein had noticed a man wearing a red kerchief, speaking to others, and organizing relief centers. Allison knew she had found where her son truly was that day and how many lives he connected with. Allison would unite with those Welles saved; Ling and Judy were among the twelve. When Allison showed them a picture of Welles, they confirmed that he was the man they saw.

Welles's parents found closure in knowing that even though their son's life may have been cut very short, a legacy was created. He died doing what he truly felt complete doing—helping people. His father recalls Welles mentioning that he felt there was something bigger he was meant to do with his life (other than working in an office). Welles possibly wanted to switch jobs and join the fire department.

Welles's story shows us that everything happens for a reason. His interest and training in the junior fire department prepared him well for the stamina and rescuing tactics he used on 9/11. His interest in constantly wearing and keeping his red bandanna with him enabled Welles to live long enough to block out the smoke, fire, and fumes to save more lives. He was a beacon of hope to those he helped. Welles listened to his intuition and life purpose, which allowed him to unite with others who needed him. They would not have known how to escape that day if not for Welles. Finding purpose through all this reveals that it's not a shame that his life was lost while saving others. His purpose was to save many others who also had a purpose to finish.

The second part of the transitioning period will help explain why you needn't let your perception of death block out any communication with your loved ones.

Your Departed Loved One's Healing Process

A life that was taken too soon—or even if it was expected—can sometimes be shocking. Even though we might not physically see or hear our loved ones, their souls never die. Doreen Virtue—best-selling author, clairvoyant, and intuitive with the angelic realm for twenty-five years—is able to channel messages from the angels and explain the life of the soul. She explains that we are all made of soul energy. When the physical body ceases, the soul doesn't.

The transition of the soul departing from the body is painless, which has been verified by those who have undergone near-death encounters. There is a sense of liberty, and the soul doesn't bear the same physical suffering that it once had. Doreen Virtue also reveals that those who have passed away haven't completely vanished; they have shifted to a much higher vibrational-energy frequency. We all emit different vibrational-energy frequencies, and when we think about those we have lost, we are connecting our frequencies.

When you think about your loved ones, don't worry about their safety or well-being. They are in a much better place now. They have let go of the earthly limitations of the mind. They are getting healthier, restoring their energy, and continuing to live on with God. Any unresolved forgiveness matters between you and your grandparent(s) may block the necessary healing and communication. It's crucial to send loving thoughts and prayers for their healing as they transition.

What Are They Accomplishing?

Time is calculated very differently in heaven. What might seem like an eternity here on earth is seconds in heaven. When it seems like it's been a while since you've felt contact, your loved ones may be accomplishing one or all of the following:

❖ undergoing much-needed self-care
❖ learning and gaining new insights into what they have accomplished on earth (also known as a "life review")
❖ preparing to return to earth through reincarnation for another lifetime (if they choose) to heal karmic paths

Doreen Virtue affirms that each of us has our own unique heavenly path designed for the soul's growth. Those who don't believe in life after death may be surprised when consciousness still thrives. They must rest in the afterlife while they come to terms with knowing the soul carries on. This could take as long as it needs to. Those who have had harrowing deaths may need extensive healing in heaven before they are prepared to connect with family and friends.

James Van Praagh, author and spiritual medium for thirty years, has the ability to channel and connect with those who have passed away. He recounts how loved ones are not alone when they pass away. Their guardian angels are with them during this process. Others from the past are waiting to greet them in heaven to aid in the self-care process. Sometimes the passing of a loved one is violent or quick, which leaves the departed feeling confused and needing time to realize what has happened. Guardian angels will aid them through the death transition, which may require time before they can make contact on the physical plane. Your loved one may not be fully aware of how to spiritually connect with you, but their self-care will lead them to that point eventually.

According to James Van Praagh, those who have passed away from various illnesses or accidents chose their paths long before they came to earth. Based on his connection with spirit, he has found that nothing is coincidental. A soul, or group of souls, decides before coming to earth the experiences they will have together. It is part of a karmic obligation or a level of spiritual growth the soul must undergo.

These occurrences are chosen to try to equal things out, especially with illness or disease. James Van Praagh finds that those who experienced high-risk ailments decide to do so before coming here. They want to overcome and break the link so it will burn out within the family history.

We are all here to love unconditionally and to learn or experience the various avenues of life. We choose purposes that reflect unconditional love. This spiritual plan enables us to experience the good and the less than favorable situations we come across in life. James Van Praagh believes one must experience the negative aspects of life to better embrace the positive. He calls this the *duality of nature*. He also adds that the soul's mission is to wholeheartedly incorporate love in all that we do in order to return successfully to heaven.

James reveals that while in spirit, certain souls agree to undergo natural disasters, plane crashes, and other situations in which they leave their bodies suddenly. It may be hard to fathom why those we loved were taken away so soon, but they may be finishing the karmic parts of their lives and developing their souls.

Your loved ones' missions have been filled—despite their young ages when they passed. We are all here for a certain time to perform what is needed toward our purpose and our spiritual enhancement. Your lifetime is a collection of positive and negative thoughts, actions, and choices. You are reincarnated (as many times as you wish) into certain social settings, global locations, situations, and opportunities to learn from the choices you have made. Karma is energy you emanate into the world. You can compare it to the blueprint of your original purpose (part of your spiritual growth). We all incarnate at different levels depending upon where we are on our spiritual paths—pertaining to our thoughts, deeds, and actions on earth.

You forever evolve and are constantly learning from challenges you face. You share the teachings of heaven with the world. For James Van Praagh, earth is like a schoolroom where karmic paths use vital lessons of love, forgiveness, honesty, compassion, and trust to create experiences. The various careers you have reflect and showcase this purpose.

Various incarnations, help you interact with others who will also incorporate these lessons and enhance your spiritual growth. You may find that the same life lesson needs to be addressed throughout your soul journey, and it will keep occurring in each lifetime if you don't address it and heal from it right away. Any habits or patterns you notice could be a sign for you to tend to your karmic journey.

Your life review, which is accompanied by your spirit guides, assesses what you have accomplished and what you still need to learn or work on. This is performed each time you go home to heaven (before your next life). This helps further the necessary healing that needs to be done in the transitioning process.

Through the next five chapters, I will:

- ❖ Take you on a journey through my grandparent's lives,
- ❖ Describe how they still impact my life today—from heaven.
- ❖ Share with you, various methods of how you can still keep contact with yours

Let Your Healing Begin…

CHAPTER IV

With Papa, Tic Tacs Solved Everything

A grandfather is someone with silver in his hair and gold in his heart.

—Anonymous

In Ragusa, Sicily, my grandfather, Angelo Giovanni Gulino, entered the world on September 24, 1914. Papa would later experience and contribute so much to the world. He had one older brother, Giuseppe (Joseph), and two younger sisters, Giovanna (Joanna) and Nunziatina (Nancy). Papa married Rose DiPasquale and had only one child, my father, John.

Papa grew up in Ragusa, worked as a tailor, and moved to America on October 4, 1949. This date is one of many things I learned while composing this book. I researched my grandfather's name on Ancestry. com. After signing up for the free trial, a gateway revealed something special. Via a New York passenger list, I was able to uncover the name of the Italian boat my grandfather traveled on to America (The *Vulcania*). With chills running up and down my arms and a smile from ear to ear, I recognized that the documentation in front of me matched the exact information my cousin Marco had relayed to me from Italy two weeks earlier. I saw Papa's name and record index details:

Name: Gulino, Giovanni Angelo
Port of Departure: Naples
Port of Arrival: New York, New York
Date: October 4, 1949

While living in Brooklyn, New York, he was employed at a Manhattan factory that fashioned bathing suits. During the off season, he would find jobs painting, roofing, or cementing. A tall, slender man, he dressed in stylish suits and hats or dress shirts and slacks. He drove a 1964 Chevy Impala sports sedan with crimson vinyl seats and a spotless black exterior.

His care of the garden in my old backyard in Brooklyn was as gentle and loving as his demeanor. Papa took pride in tending to his eggplants, peppers, tomatoes, cucumbers, and Swiss chard, (a leafy green vegetable often used in Mediterranean cooking.) The trees consisted of figs, peaches, and apples. Papa also cultivated vines of cantaloupes. I remember looking down from my bedroom window and seeing how the afternoon sunlight would dance on the tops of his fruit trees, shimmering through the leaves.

During Papa's free time, he spent time with me, played cards, and watched WWF wrestling, witnessing the likes of Hulk Hogan and Rowdy Roddy Piper. Papa would also help maintain my father's electric trains in the basement. He also liked forming huge crosses out of the palms we received during Palm Sunday Mass. My father still has some of Papa's beautiful crosses.

Putting the Pieces Together

A fragment of my grandfather's past I never knew—and wished he was still alive to inquire about in greater detail—was his involvement in the military. The Germans captured him during World War II. My father recounted some of these intriguing stories, but I needed more information.

While composing this book and trying to decipher my grandfather's history, I felt intuitively guided by Papa. My clairsentience kicked in when I asked him to help me understand his past. I felt him urging me on and giving me the idea to reach out to my family in Sicily. The goal was to ask his sister, Nunziatina, for answers. I e-mailed my cousin Marco in Sicily to help with this—since he had access to a computer. I listened to Papa's guidance, and Marco and Nunziatina provided rare glimpses into the man I had only known as an older man.

I received photos of young and old moments in Papa's life. I saw what his life was like in the military and in Brooklyn. It brought tears to my eyes.

If a picture is worth a thousand words, I had more than that! Some of the pictures, which you will notice throughout this chapter, have enabled me to connect with him on a whole new level. When I look at the photos, his smile still portrays his love for me. Within his eyes, I feel him saying hello in each image. I hear him saying, "I'm here, and I never left."

Memories of War

In his early twenties, Papa was in the Italian army. He served in Italy, Albania, Greece, and Ethiopia. In 1936, Ethiopia was a colony of Italy and was occupied by them as well. During that time, there were hopes of turning the area into an economic asset. Investments were made in creating infrastructures such as roads, airports, hospitals, and colonizing farm areas.

Papa was in the military service during World War II (1939-1945), which had some of the darkest highlights of that time: The Holocaust (1941-1945), the bombing of Pearl Harbor (1941), and the atomic bombing of Hiroshima, (1945). When Italy surrendered in 1943, the Germans took Papa prisoner. Until the end of the war in 1945, Papa was used as a laborer in different locations. He may have been asked to prepare for invasions, build roads, and bolster German defenses. My grandfather witnessed many horrific events.

In the German work camps, daily attendance was taken. It was made clear that if your name was called and you didn't respond—or if your name was called and you were missing—you would be shot when you were found. One time, Papa's name was called first, and he was so nervous that he didn't hear his name. When his name was called a second time, his friend nudged Papa and said, "That's you!" My grandfather hastily confirmed that he was present. Papa and the others in the group were fearful for their lives during that time.

When marching or riding in trucks, my grandfather and the other prisoners had to get off sometimes to take cover from artillery shells and aerial attacks. They had to hug the ground as close as possible. One member of the group was so scared that he started to run toward what he thought was safer ground. The other prisoners pleaded for him to stay down, but the restless gentleman didn't listen. When he moved, one of the shells killed him.

Food consisted basically of scraps and watery soup. A decent meal was very rare. A treat would consist of string beans and potatoes. My father said that was why he still loved and appreciated string beans and potatoes. When he was a child, he refused to eat them—until his mother told him Papa's stories. It changed my father's perspective entirely.

When the group arrived at a camp in Germany, they were told to take showers. Papa and the others were afraid because rumors were swirling that they would be executed in the shower area. However, when they entered the showers, the water was running. The German soldiers brought them soap, towels, and clean clothes. Papa and the other prisoners were all relieved, thanking God for another day alive.

When Germany surrendered in 1945, my grandfather returned to Sicily with a blanket and barely any clothes. My grandfather never liked to watch war movies on TV or talk much about the war.

Papa: My Strength, Protection, and Best Friend

April 19, 2002, was a radiant day. There was not a cloud in the sky. It was warm enough to leave the house with just a blue denim jacket. My hair was still wet from my shower, without catching a draft. I was presenting a speech for a class at Wagner College in Staten Island, New York. It was my graduation year.

The drive from Brooklyn was about thirty minutes. I passed through the Belt Parkway on my way to the Verrazano Narrows Bridge. The never-ending construction was a personal favorite of all the residents. On route, you'll always find an impatient New Yorker who's insulted by your lack of "not speeding as if a bat was chasing you," and undeniably cut you off in spite of it. A similar driver passed me by, and I remember frustratingly saying to myself, *Geez! What's the rush?* I changed lanes without knowing that those few seconds it took to switch on my turn signal and blink my eyes would feel like an eternity.

I didn't realize how sloppy and uneven the pavement was from the highway construction. The tires of my black Toyota Camry somehow got tangled in that choppy mess. I abruptly and uncontrollably swerved diagonally all the way to the side of the highway. In utter disbelief, I looked in my rearview mirror. The cars behind me were determined to reach their destinations—no matter what was in their path. A flood of panic drowned me. I was alone in the car—and I had never felt so isolated. I thought, *I don't have time for this.*

Papa and I at the dining room table in my old apartment

Papa and I were always together; that for a while I had developed an Italian accent. He lived downstairs from my top-floor apartment in Brooklyn, and I made every opportunity to see him daily. We were best buds, and as a young child, we shared many valuable moments. We cooked together, and Papa didn't mind when I scraped off the special, seasoned-breadcrumb garnish he placed over his pork chop dishes. We would have dessert together, and I loved playing with the red and white bakery string from the box of the delectable Italian cookies. I washed it down with a smidgen of coffee, which I don't drink as an adult. If he were still alive today, I wonder if I would request espresso trips at Dunkin Donuts or bakeries?

Papa always had the gentlest ways of comforting me, especially when I scraped my knees while running outside one summer. When I had stomachaches, he would place me on his lap, rock me back and forth, and give me Tic Tacs. As an adult, I found out that peppermint was great for soothing the stomach. I always felt protected and safe near him. I knew that everything would be okay. If I had an accident during my toilet-training years, he had extra undergarments for me to change into. Until I could walk on my own, Papa held me lovingly and proudly, and he continues to hold me today…

Before I could think, the air bag exploded. The other cars were nowhere to be found. It was as if someone just swished and flicked a magic wand from Hogwarts and transported all the cars to another dimension.

The highway was all mine, but I wasn't to remain idle. After the first impact, my car proceeded toward the left side of the highway, slamming harshly into the guardrail. The bag exploded around the lower part of my face. I felt stinging near my mouth. I thought some skin had come off. Simultaneously as the powdery substance from the bag was deployed, my body was held back, and my right arm, raised up. All the missing cars behind me then returned and passed the wreckage.

Without hesitation, I jumped out of the car, fearing that it might explode from a gas leak. As I exited, I noticed the hood was dented. The engine fell to the ground. As I turned to the left, I saw shocked faces running along the Belt Parkway path by the water. Their stunned faces said, *"How can someone just jump out of a collision like that with nothing broken?"*

Then it hit me … hard — the piercing, throbbing sensation I had felt was from an extreme abrasion that radiated from the most sensitive part of my arm-under my bicep. It looked like a slice of pepperoni.

After my hospital visit, I rehashed the day's horrific events on the drive home with my parents. The one memory that crept back in was how my body went back in my seat and how my right arm raised. It was as if someone from the backseat held my body back and lifted my arm in a particular way to prevent further damage. I instantly knew that Papa was keeping me safe, protected, and alive. It wasn't my time to leave yet, and he would help me heal. If he were still alive, I could see him giving me Tic Tacs. Even though I was in my twenties, I would probably feel that eating them would have made things better too.

Helen Keller said, "What we have once enjoyed, we can never lose. All that we love deeply becomes a part of us."

Timeless Gifts

My grandfather died on October 20, 1984, of a heart attack. I was only four years old and too young to fully understand the sadness that follows death. My parents told me he was in heaven and safe with Jesus. I felt comforted to know that.

Papa's passing weighed heavy on everyone. He was such a patient, calm, understanding, and loving person. There was not a bad bone in his body. He had no bad habits. We never needed to worry when Papa was around, and he always made us feel complete. My mother appreciated how peaceful he was to be around and how he was always so helpful while he was looking after me. I see a lot of Papa in my father. He has the same gentleness, unconditional love, and kind, generous spirit.

When you look into the mirror, you can see your grandparents. Their past is your future. Papa leaves all these beautiful emotions behind. For me, he has left his gifts of patience (everything in divine timing), security (that I will always be protected, I'm never alone), strength (to never be afraid of the unknown—to move forward fearlessly), and serenity (to always remember the peace from within my soul). These characteristics/qualities are a part of me. Because of him, I try every day to live them to the best of my ability.

In Chapter VII, I will discuss in more depth, how Papa has connected with me through the years along with Grandma Marie. For Grandma Rose, I will discuss my communication style with her in Chapter VI.

CHAPTER V

XYZ, Grandma Marie!

Somewhere over the rainbow, way up high there's a land that I heard of, once in a lullaby. Somewhere, over the rainbow, skies are blue and the dreams that you dare to dream really do come true.

—"Over the Rainbow", lyrics by Edgar Yipsel Harbug, composed by Harold Arlen

Grandma Marie would always sing "Over the Rainbow" to her six grandchildren. Every time she did, it was with great passion. My love for the 1939 movie, *The Wizard of Oz* grew stronger because of her. I

still think of her when this movie is on TV or if I pass by a store that sells its memorabilia.

Grandma would sing the famous nursery rhymes—"London Bridge is Falling Down," "Itsy Bitsy Spider," "Ring Around the Rosie," and "Where is Thumbkin?"—and we would act out each and every song. She never tired of repeating whichever song I wanted to hear.

My later memories of her singing were Italian melodies. Whether it was at family weddings or visiting in her Brooklyn apartment, I was always guaranteed to be serenaded. Even when she was in the nursing home, she never forgot the lyrics of her favorite tunes.

Her fondness for singing started when she was a little girl. Grandma Marie was very close with her father and would always spend time with him. Sometimes he would have her sing in Italian and dance for those he knew. Those who watched were always entertained and fascinated by the young girl who was able to sing in another language.

For our wedding reception, Grandma Marie performed one last time. My husband Anthony and I wanted to include a video montage of our grandparents who had passed away and couldn't physically be there on our wedding day. Spiritually, we knew they attended. Anthony and I felt, the need to honor our grandparents so strongly; our entire families wouldn't be present without them.

The video started with Grandma Marie singing "My Love Forgive Me (Amore Scusami)" by Vito Pallavicini and Gino Mescoli. It may not have been a typical song to have played at a wedding, but it was the only Italian song I had recorded her singing. It was a precious surprise for everyone since we had kept it a surprise during our wedding preparations. When we heard her voice filling the venue, it was as if she was with us all once more.

Growing Up

Marie Ruggiero was born on March 28, 1920 in Queens, New York, and was the youngest among three sisters and one brother. Grandma Marie loved to read when she was a child—and well into her eighties. She would read more than three hundred pages of various genres in two days! When she was little, Grandma would sneak off to the library—without her mother knowing—and relish in whatever book interested her there. As I got older, I inherited her love of reading. I could get lost in in a Barnes & Noble. I love reading so much that I would like to have the Treehouse Masters from the Animal Planet construct a cozy library-cabin tree house for me. Grandma Marie was also very good with math and did well in school. Grandma was interested in becoming a nurse and could have been one with her high grades. However, when her father died (before she was eighteen), she had to quit school to help her family at home. In later years, she took up stenography and worked as a salesperson in a children's store, as a worker in a bag/shoe factory, and as a babysitter.

In her ninety-one years, she lived through the presidential terms of Franklin Roosevelt, John F. Kennedy, and Ronald Reagan, the landing on the moon, and fashion changes. Grandma Marie was the oldest living grandparent I had—and the one I have the most memories of.

There is one significant period of time she lived through, The Great Depression that I feel taught her perseverance, strength, and survival quality. During the Great Depression, there was a worldwide economic decline, which occurred when the stock market crashed on October 29, 1929. It was a domino effect of: people trying to sell stocks that no one purchased, banks that invested in client's savings—then closing their doors, people withdrawing their money out of fear from the banks closing, others going bankrupt when they couldn't take out their savings in time, and farm owners experiencing dust storms, also known as the Dust Bowl; that destroyed crops. To say it was a rough time was an understatement. My mother recounts Grandma telling her that during the Depression, most of the meals consisted of pasta, soup, beans, and vegetables.

Grandma's strength and determination carried over into her morning routine in later years. She would get up by seven and start cleaning, shopping, doing laundry, cooking, and climbing up and down flights of stairs with groceries and other heavy items. She continued this into her early eighties. Grandma also had mighty physical strength, despite her age. When she held my hand, despite her arthritis, she still had a strong grip! I felt lingering pressure after she let go, but it just showed how much love she had for me. My mom would always say, "They just don't make them like that anymore."

Grandma Marie had a tendency to buy produce and other groceries in extreme bulk. I feel it was a developed habit to ensure she always had what she needed due to the Great Depression. My family and I would sometimes look in her closets and jokingly ask, "Is there a blizzard heading our way that we aren't unaware of?" The tons of napkins, toilet paper, and paper towels in her closet were reminiscent of the way Costco stocked its shelves.

Grandma Marie also lived through decades of great musicians: Frank Sinatra, Jerry Vale, Jimmy Roselli, and Lou Monte. She was a huge Yankees fan and devoted time to watching the best on TV: Mickey Mantle, Graig Nettles, Lou Piniella, Willie Randolph, and Derek Jeter.

Grandma enjoyed watching *Jeopardy,* (an American game show where contestants are quizzed on general knowledge) and *Wheel of Fortune* (an American game show where contestants solve word puzzles for cash and prizes.) Grandma Marie relished in viewing famous comedy duos, including Laurel and Hardy and Abbott and Costello. Laurel and Hardy were well-known for their slapstick comedy from 1920-1940's. I preferred Abbott and Costello. They were renowned for their Vaudeville acts in 1935, stage, film and television appearances, in the 1940's and 1950's. Their legendary skit, *Who's on First?* is worth viewing on the internet, to fully appreciate their comic genius. Grandma Marie also frequently watched another favorite classic of mine, *The Honeymooners,* a sitcom set in Brooklyn New York in the 1950's, depicting the lives of two married couples and the working class, staring Jackie Gleason. Grandma Marie loved a good laugh, which was inevitable when watching these shows. I'd always laugh with her as well.

My Pen Pal

> *Grandma always made you feel she had been waiting to see just you all day and now the day was complete.*

—Marcy DeMaree

I began writing this chapter around two important dates: her birthday in heaven (she would have been ninety-five in March 2015) and Palm Sunday. On Palm Sunday, Grandma would always tell me the story of how she almost wasn't named Marie. *(Palm Sunday is celebrated through Christian tradition as a holiday remembering when Jesus entered into Jerusalem before he had suffered and died on the cross. It is associated with the blessing and procession of palms from local trees that the crowd scattered in front of Jesus as he rode into Jerusalem.)* As the story goes, Grandma was born on Palm Sunday, and her mother had wanted to name her "Palma" after the holiday. However, her mother was persuaded not to.

This connection between the timing of the holiday and writing this chapter to some may seem like a coincidence, rather it's another sign that Grandma Marie is still connecting with me and letting me know her interest in sharing this with you all. I definitely felt her appreciation and willingness to be present while I was composing this book. In life, there are no coincidences; there are merely divine-timing moments that work together in perfect harmony.

I miss driving to visit Grandma Marie after my classes in college and my weekend visits to her Brooklyn apartment. In the summer, her apartment was always so cool and refreshing. She kept all her windows open, a benefit of living right by the water. In the winter, her heat was always cranked high. Some people thought it was stifling, but I felt as if I was wrapped in a comforting blanket.

During my visits, we would sometimes sit at her round kitchen table with scrolled, high-back café looking chairs, and talked about our days' events. Sometimes she would have me talk to her close friend on the phone. Grandma must have talked about me a lot to her friend because she was always so happy to hear from me. I remember Grandma's friend always told me that it was so thoughtful that I made time to see Grandma Marie.

Conversations with Grandma though were a bit challenging at times since Grandma didn't hear very well. When she was pregnant with my mother Sandy, she had a cold and couldn't take any medication. Her hearing grew progressively worse, and she needed a hearing aid. Our conversations sometimes turned into comical scenes. I would say, *"Grandma, how are you feeling today?"* She would answer, *"It looks like rain outside."*

If I asked her a specific question that needed a detailed answer, she would just look at me, nod, and smile. I knew it wasn't the answer I was looking for.

When it was time to eat, Grandma Marie would always ensure there was enough food to eat. She would sometimes make potato and eggs on a roll, my absolute favorite dish. It was simple to prepare, but she fried it in the pan, cooked the potatoes crispy and used the right amount of

Parmesan cheese, which made all the difference. My second favorite meal she cooked was lentil soup with elbow pasta. It was the ultimate comfort food, especially on a brutal winter day. A sprinkle of Parmesan cheese topped it off just right. Her beef stews were packed with string beans, corn, peas, carrots, cubed potatoes, stew beef, tomato paste, beef broth, and other herbs.

On the days she didn't cook, she would order pizza from Pizza Den on Eighteenth Avenue in Brooklyn. We absolutely loved eating their Sicilian slices, which always had the right consistency of crust thickness, flavorful tomato sauce, gooey cheese, and fresh basil. I recall her having pizza with Coca-Cola in a white, pale blue, and pink floral tea cup. *(A different way to enjoy the crisp beverage, I know, but it was her thing.)* One particular time I remember grandma drinking soda from the cup was when my sister Jana and I were playing the card game War. In a teasing fashion, I suggested the enticing game of "52-Card Pickup." When Jana agreed to play, she was disappointed to find that picking up all fifty-two cards from the floor was not the kind of card game she had in mind. Grandma drinking from "the cup," tried not to laugh too much, and she suggested refraining from such a game request.

Grandma Marie in her apartment with my sister, Jana

When I sat at Grandma's dining room table, each place setting had a stack of napkins and lots of silverware—even if it wasn't a meal that called for it. I couldn't help but express my amusement, especially when she would offer other foods during the meal. If we were having dinner, she would offer a sandwich, a banana or yogurt. If we didn't eat at Grandma Marie's house, Jana and I would take Grandma to IHOP in Staten Island, a restaurant known for their tasty pancakes, hash browns, waffles crepes and more.

When we didn't see each other, Grandma Marie and I would schedule time to talk on the phone. Fridays at eight was our time slot. It was such a special time in my life with her, and I will cherish it forever. I was able to speak to her about whatever happened during the day, the weather, and all kinds of other things. I wish I could pick up the phone and do it all again. It sometimes was a bit hard to talk on the phone because of her hearing aid. It made the conversations more entertaining when I had to repeat everything five thousand times. I can still hear her laughing hysterically because she knew she didn't hear me, but I still had patience through it all. I miss her hearty merriment.

When we weren't speaking on the phone, we wrote letters to each other. When I was younger, my letters were more frequent. As I grew older, I didn't get the chance to write as much—but she still did. She always addressed me as her "pen pal," and we would sign off with "XYZ!" This was a reminder of when we sang the ABCs together. She would say, "XYZ!" really fast, and I would giggle hysterically. It was her special way of saying "I love you!" I would close the letter by writing, "I got it!" Whenever I was about to leave her apartment, she would ask if I had everything. I would shout, "I got it!" She would always give a hearty chuckle to my response. I miss her laugher.

Treasured Attributes

The last few years of Grandma Marie's life involved many trips to an assisted living home and hospice care. It was rough for my family to see Grandma needing assistance to do all the things she used to do on her own. However, a severe fall in her apartment proved that she couldn't live on her own much longer. It was safer for her to be in the care of those who could provide for her 24/7. I know it was especially hard for my mother, and she wondered if she had made the right decision to place her in assistant living. We reassured her it was for the best, due to the circumstances at hand.

Toward the end, Grandma Marie suffered slight dementia, kidney problems, and pneumonia. She passed away peacefully in her sleep on March 12, 2011, from congestive heart failure. She was survived by three children, six grandchildren, and nine great-grandchildren. Grandma Marie had especially close bonds with each of her grandchildren, which I know they will never forget.

Her husband had passed away from Alzheimer's disease on February 14, 1984. Grandma's perseverance made its appearance again during her eighteen years of caring for Grandpa Larry. In the eighties, services for Alzheimer's weren't available as much as they are today. Due to his condition, I didn't see much of Grandpa Larry and have no recollection of him. I wonder what our relationship would have been like if things were different.

Grandma leaves behind the gift of being young at heart. No matter how old she was, she still looked young. No one could ever believe her age. She always looked like she was in her early sixties. Grandma Marie was always spontaneous and full of merriment—even though she experienced some rough times in her life. She taught me to always smile, laugh, and express myself creatively through my writing.

Grandma Marie forever has a place in my heart. Her name is part of my middle name: "Rosemarie." "Rose" is for my other grandmother. My middle name encompasses the beauty of both women who meant so very much to me in their own unique ways.

If I have a daughter, I will pass along this middle name. I will sing all the nursery rhymes Grandma Marie taught me with exuberant energy. I will show my daughter that no matter what age you are, there's no better feeling than having a smile in your heart.

Someday I'll wish upon a star and wake up where the clouds are far behind me. Where troubles melt like lemon drops away above the chimney tops, that's where you'll find me. Somewhere, over the rainbow.

—"Over the Rainbow"

CHAPTER VI

Grandma Rose: Reflections of Me

A garden of love grows in a grandmother's heart.

—Author unknown

Have you ever met someone and felt as if you've known the person forever? Some relationships take several years of getting to know one another before there is a tight bond. However, other relationships require less time to generate the same attachment. Take this magnitude of emotions and place it with the scenario of someone you've never met on this physical plane. This is my unique relationship with Grandma Rose.

On December 8, 1976, Grandma Rose passed away at St. Luke's Hospital in Houston. She suffered from rheumatic heart disease and had flown to Houston from Brooklyn to receive the proper care for her condition. After open-heart surgery left her weak, heart failure claimed her life. I was born four years later. My father John says his mother and I have many similarities. This is where our connection begins…

Beginnings

Rose DiPasquale was born on February 4, 1914, in the Lower East Side of Manhattan, NY. Her address was 27–29 Monroe Street, and the building she was born in, still stands today! It was almost torn down when the Alfred E. Smith Housing Project was constructed across the street. The development was completed in 1953 and was named after the four-time New York governor. Alfred E. Smith fought for better living conditions in New York City. His legislature provided better housing, improved child welfare, better factory conditions, and more state parks.

Grandma Rose's parents, Angelo and Rosaria, came to America in the early 1900s from Sicily. Her only sister died at a very young age of an unknown illness. Grandma Rose also had a brother. She was an American citizen and didn't live on Monroe Street long. When World War I started in 1914, her father Angelo was called to service in Sicily. She grew up in Ragusa, and Papa and Grandma Rose lived in the same neighborhood. They all knew each other well. Grandma Rose was seven months older than Papa.

After some time, her brother Joe went back to America to prepare for the family's return. Grandma Rose returned to America in the 1930s. She and my great-grandmother Rosaria (Grandma DiPasquale, as my family called her) worked in the garment industry. After World War II, Grandma Rose returned to Sicily. During this extended visit, the relationship between Grandma Rose and Papa grew. They wed in November 1948. She returned to the United States in January 1949.

Grandma Rose with Papa and my father John

***

It's rare to come across anyone who remembers specific details about his or her great-grandmother. I was very blessed to have had the opportunity to share some time with Grandma DiPasquale. Ages four through eight are my fondest and simplest memories of Grandma. She was in her nineties. I recall the pink and white checkered apron with floral patterns she sewed for me, playing with her black rotary phone, eating lemon drop candies. As I typed this line, the aroma of freshly cut orange peels surrounded me, which I automatically knew was Grandma DiPasquale's way of reminding me through clear feeling (receiving messages through smell) about the times we would eat this juicy, sweet fruit together.

I had fun folding the dinner napkins in triangles at her ivory kitchen table. Sometimes for dinner, if my father wasn't home to grill hamburgers, she would make chicken and rice. The rice unfortunately wasn't my favorite; it was quite watery since she could not eat foods with seasoning. However, as I look back at those dinner visits with her downstairs from my apartment, I wish I could have those rare moments in time with her again. Grandma DiPasquale passed away on September 25, 1988 (a month after my sister, Jana, was born) at the age of ninety-six. She fell in the kitchen while opening the refrigerator door. Her hip bone was brittle and needed surgery. After receiving a hip replacement and going to a nursing home, she became ill and passed away a week later.

My many visits with Grandma DiPasquale after school should have warranted her an award for putting up with my slightly mischievous ways. I would walk by her and tug at her multicolored, long-sleeved dress, and I would wave something past her thin, white hair so it would stick up. The best was when I decided to use her walls and couches as a canvas instead of coloring with crayons on paper. Through it all, she would smile and laugh with amusement. I guess that's the great love of a great-grandmother. I miss her so.

Grandma Rose (on the left) and her mother—
my great grandmother DiPasquale

*Photo taken of myself at my bridal shower
that reminds me of Grandma Rose*

Virtues Shared—Staying Connected

Poise, self-assurance, and compassion were the natural fibers that composed Grandma Rose's being. Elegant in every way, she always dressed with impeccable style and matched with the greatest of detail. From her fashionable hats to sophisticated gloves, Grandma Rose always complemented her dresses with the finest accessories—without breaking the bank to do so.

When looking at photographs of her, I see our comparable tastes reflected in how I dress today. I too find myself balancing my entire ensemble with coordinating colors, fabrics, and shoes. I notice my interest in women's clothing from the 1940s, which is another way I bond with Grandma Rose. My father frequently tells me that I look so much like her. Now that I'm getting older, my smile, walk, and posture make my father do double-takes. I'm so honored to be able to resemble her, especially since I never met her. All I have to do is look in the mirror, and she's there.

My clairsentience conveys that she was a woman who spoke with the highest integrity, set the truest intentions in life, and believed in being assertive in a loving manner. I detect that the energy of my grandmother was rare even for her time—just as it is for me in this current era. The way I interpret matters in life and my moral compass vary from the majority. I never judge others for their choices in life *(to each his/her own)*. I do find that I choose different paths than most.

As I forge ahead in all areas of my life, I feel Grandma Rose instill, with the help of my angels, the importance of self-worth, remembering who I am, and aligning with my purpose. I understand this more now that I'm thirty-five, and it's so liberating. I've come so far from being a shy, self-conscious girl. I was very uncomfortable in my own skin for so long, and I couldn't see the value of my own uniqueness. Over the years, everything I've experienced has shaped me into the person I am today. For this, I'm forever grateful.

My connection with God, Jesus, and my guardian angels also grew stronger and made me appreciate the divine spark within me. I ascertained that the rough patches weren't a curse; they were blessings in disguise. Those pieces of the bigger picture permitted me to assess more of who I want to be, and revealed that I deserve to acquire the best for my life. I know that through time, there will be more levels of inner workings that I will explore, as the evolution of the self never ceases.

Grandma Rose and I believe in defending what is right, having a voice, and being respectable. I had trouble with confrontations while I was growing up. No one wants to discuss sensitive matters with someone if they're afraid the relationship might suffer because of it. How you approach things matters, and your honest intentions make all the difference. Be honest about how you feel and let everything out on the table.

In all relationships, there are instances when you've tried to handle a situation gently, but the other person reacts in a negative manner. If you attempted to reconcile and still see zero positive changes in the status of the relationship—or willingness on the other person's part to make amends—then the best you can do is wish the other person well in his or her life. You must move on confidently from the situation.

Even though ending certain relationships may be complicated, it is needed for healing on both sides—and for your progression for what's yet to come on your journey. For example, friends in kindergarten, junior high, and high school used to mirror your interests. However, as you both ventured through life, transitions started to emerge. You're both not the same, because you are experiencing life differently and at your own pace.

Changes in friendships are natural. You grow and evolve into different personalities, which doesn't make either person bad. We all have different interests and must follow our own paths. Some paths lead together—and some don't. The friendships you once had were right for the moment in time they served, but there comes a point when you must interact with those who mirror your best intentions. Move forward by confidently trusting that God will bring these relationships back healed or deliver new ones that are better attuned to your current well-being.

After channeling my thoughts and notes about Grandma Rose, I asked my father about his memories of his mother. She died when he was twenty-six, and it was tough for him to remember so far back. However, some of his recollections were identical to mine, which was proof that I was channeling her character. She always taught him to be respectable to others, to talk matters out, and to be honest with his true feelings. She was very generous to those she knew and opened her house to many, creating loving memories. My father, with a grateful demeanor, also divulged that Grandma Rose taught him how to cook, clean, and be responsible at a young age. She felt it was necessary for him to have experience in these areas in case his future wife became ill. My father has commendable, gentlemanly qualities and is such an honorable man because of what Grandma Rose shared with him.

I recognize that Grandma Rose extended her confidence in me to pursue my writing dreams, motivated me to help others through my angel readings, and encouraged me to share inspirational stories that will provide comfort to many. It might seem hard to fathom how a person would recognize where this wisdom is coming from, especially when it's linked with someone you've never met before, but you can't shake the sensation. It's a truthful burning from within that you just know not to question. When you channel the energies of others, you identify it as authentic. For me, believing is seeing.

Grandma Rose and Papa in their apartment

CHAPTER VII

You're Not Imagining It—They Are Sending You Messages

From earlier Chapters, I shared some of the ways my grandparents have connected with me such as Papa saving my life during my car accident, to Grandma Marie hugging me days after she had passed away. In this Chapter, I will reveal more ways that I have recognized their presence. First, let's quickly recap what you need to know in order to connect with your loved ones:

It's important to remember to clear and forgive yourself of any fear, doubt, or guilt, etc., you may have had toward your grandparents' passing, or the relationship you may have had in general with them. These lower emotions as discussed earlier in this book, will only mute the connection that is trying to come through. If need be, please refer back to Chapters I and II, so as to ensure you are ready/willing to feel the connection you are seeking.

Please know that you are deserving of receiving your grandparents' loving messages, and if you allow yourself to think otherwise, you'll also find it difficult to make contact with them. You have more intuitive abilities than you realize, and the guidance you are given, comes from a trustworthy source. This source always feels loving, gentle and secure.

If you have done all you could on your part to prepare yourself for a connection with your grandparents, and still have yet to connect, remember that they are going through a healing transitioning period as well. Please refer to Chapter III to review this process.

Ask and You Shall Receive….

Your angels are constantly guiding and watching over you. However, your free will still determines the depth of how much your angels can intervene in your life. You still have a choice regarding how much contact your angels have with you. The more you pray/talk to them, the more they are invited into your world—and the more you're able to identify their guiding energy around you.

It's also important to be clear and truly state your intentions when having a dialogue with God and your angels. Be honest with yourself. Don't hold back! You're never bothering them, and no question or request is big or small enough to take them away from helping others. God and your angels are present at all times for everyone! When something is troubling you or you need advice, don't hesitate for a second to ask your angels for assistance.

When you truly ask from the depths of your soul about what you want, you are allowing outcomes to properly align to you. God and your Angels will not judge your emotions. Some people are confused though when they pray or ask for help and think their requests are going unheard. One or two things may be happening at that time. First, divine timing has yet to come into play. There are other resources or people involved that may still need to be nurtured in order to be ready to unite with your request. God and your angels see the bigger picture for you. When you are too close to a situation/goal, and place too much control in the matter, it's harder to see what truly is best. The universe will always deliver what you need. Trust this flow of abundance for you. Second, the way in which you ask for assistance makes all the difference. Does your intentions truly match with what you're asking for? Don't hold back!

Your angels encourage you to understand that there is never any harm in asking a question. The more you inquire, the further you'll develop. There is no such thing as defeat or weakness when asking for help. When you're ready to make a connection with your grandparents through sight, sound, feeling, or knowing, all you have to do is ask your loved one, God, or your angels. Always have patience and faith that your prayers will be heard soon. It may take some time before you make contact, but have faith that some form of contact will be made.

❖ God, my guardian angels, please send me strong, consistent, and familiar signs that my grandparents are well and are with me right now.

❖ (Enter grandparent name here), please send me strong, consistent, and familiar signs that you are watching over me and that you are safe and well.

You can tailor these prayers to however you are feeling at the moment when you want to connect. There is no specific prayer etiquette for speaking to your loved ones in heaven. When it comes from the heart, that's all you need.

Clear and Purify—Love and Forgive

To ensure a deeper connection and enhanced magnitude/ frequency of incoming signs, several principles can open the channels of communication. To do so requires mental and physical parts of the self, becoming centered and balanced. The mental part of self— old habits, patterns, or ways of thinking that no longer suit you—or people who drain your energy from performing your highest good must be recognized and released. These lower energies can prevent or block the flow of communicating with your angels and loved ones. To physically clear and purify, Doreen Virtue advises you to "cleanse and detoxify" your well-being, which goes way beyond exercising in the gym to get your energy flowing. For example, the less sugar and caffeine you consume, more water you drink, and healthier foods you eat, the more you boost the levels of receptivity with your grandparents/loved ones. Other important areas to clear and purify for your well-being are addictions such as smoking, drinking, or drug use. These can distort your true feelings and create a barrier between you and your divine communication.

The two important components in life are love and forgiveness—one can't go without the other. Forgiveness in others means that you no longer want to hold onto the pain you felt in a situation. You aren't justifying what the other person did; instead, you want to move forward and feel better without holding onto the hurtful emotions. You can't change anyone, but you can change how you perceive what really has happened to you and your reaction to it.

Forgiveness of yourself means that you are patient with yourself along your path of healing or understanding of something new. It's okay if you don't know everything sometimes—forgive yourself for any mistakes you've made. For in the spiritual world, mistakes don't exist; rather they are blessings in disguise. This is an opportunity to grow and learn something new about yourself. When you forgive, no matter what it's regarding, you increase the ability to love yourself, love others, and love life! Forgiveness lifts away any blocks and fears that prevent you from attracting the good and positive in your life and contact with others.

Gertrude Tooley Buckingham said, "As I kiss your pictured face so dear. As I look into your eyes so clear. I feel your presence and know you're here. And it seems I hear you speak my name.

Signs: None Too Big or Small

When you least expect it, you may get a sign from your grandparents that is packed with symbolic meaning. At other times, it arrives in the simplest form. When you need a message the most, your grandparents' presence is more powerful than you could ever imagine. When you ask to receive messages from them, there is no need to expect certain signs. Keep yourself open and receptive to the unlimited amount of ways you can receive divine communication. Let the universe send you what you need.

If you ask for specific detailed signs ("I only want to see birds to confirm my prayers of my loved ones"), then the process of what is yet to be will not reach its fullest potential. You may miss the opportunity for your soul to really grow and understand what it needs to do or experience to move forward. The signs will present themselves to you in familiar ways or in beautiful new ones.

You may find that your connections or experiences go beyond the scope of what I mention in this book, which is encouraging since we all have different stories to tell. You can have a unique communication style with your grandparents. The signs I've personally experienced in this book, which are listed below, are just the tip of the iceberg of what you can experience. You are not limited to the following:

Ways to Receive Answered Prayers/Signs

- ❖ coins on the ground
- ❖ feathers
- ❖ rainbows
- ❖ significant colors
- ❖ angelic sparkles of light
- ❖ heart-shaped clouds
- ❖ hearing a song repetitively on the radio
- ❖ overhearing a conversation that involves your situation
- ❖ reading an article
- ❖ seeing frequent numbers such as "444," "333" or other number combinations on license plates, receipts, digital clocks, or home addresses, which have a personal meaning for you
- ❖ butterflies, birds, dragonflies
- ❖ radio and/or TV turns on by itself
- ❖ smell of roses, incense, perfume, cologne, or cooking
- ❖ feeling a warm sensation (as if being hugged)
- ❖ dream visits
- ❖ visits/visions from Mother Mary or Jesus
- ❖ seeing the name of a departed grandparent in an advertisement
- ❖ hearing your name being called by a grandparent
- ❖ items in your room being misplaced or moved
- ❖ seeing visions or feeling your grandparent during your waking state

❖ finding lost items from your grandparents such as old photos, jewelry, or medals

Connecting Clairvoyantly with My Grandparents

Celebrating my birthday. In photo are my sister,
Jana, my father's cousin Salvatore, and Papa

In almost every picture I have with my grandfather, Papa was either hugging me or placing his arm around me. During one of my father's family visits from Italy, we were all able to celebrate my birthday together. I was in my early twenties, and I thought it was delightful to be able to commemorate my birthday with part of my family I didn't get to see so often.

A photo was taken of me just after blowing out my birthday candles, but the photo turned out to be more than just an ordinary one. Toward the middle portion of this photo, by the left side of my waist, there is a thin white arc, almost like an upside-down crescent moon with the curved end facing up. At first glance, some might think the white arch is a simple distortion from the photo development, but it isn't that straightforward.

I instantly knew in my heart that my grandfather was joining my family on my special day. It was Papa's way of letting me know that he wouldn't miss one birthday—even from heaven—and that he'd always be by my side.

***

When I pray or think about my grandparents, I see gorgeous brown and yellow butterflies in odd places that you normally wouldn't find them. I go on vacation to Ocean City, Maryland, quite frequently, and in all my visits, I had never seen as many butterflies as I did as I walked by the water one time. The butterflies were not flying fast; instead, they were flying at the same casual walking pace as I was. They were gliding ever so gently. It was if the butterflies were holding onto me in a loving way.

I recognized that my grandparents were making their presence known through the eyes of nature. Since I absolutely adore butterflies, it was an incredible symbol for me. Butterflies are representative of development, transformation, and renewal. When you think of a loved one who has passed away and see a butterfly, your loved one is showing you they are healthy and are doing fine.

***

After Grandma Marie passed away, I started to write letters to her in a journal. Some weeks after I wrote to her, I visited my parents for Thanksgiving. After settling down from eating the scrumptious appetizers, my father said he had something for me. When I moved out, there were some possessions I forgot to take. My father was clearing out some things I had left behind, and he stumbled upon something he knew I would find interesting. He handed me a small white envelope, and I instantly recognized the script. It was Grandma Marie's. I opened the envelope, and there was a letter inside that was addressed to me. Happy tears streamed down my face.

When I saw that the letter wasn't dated, goose bumps appeared up and down my arms. She had always dated her letters! I knew without a doubt that the letter was her way of answering my request to have contact with her from my journal writing. To see her handwriting once more—and running my fingers across each blue-inked, scripted word—was like revisiting our pen pal days.

The letter spoke of things that were actually occurring at that time, such as the cold weather and my recent plans. As a bonus, a gift of four dollars was enclosed. Grandma Marie always made sure I left her house with money for train fare or gas for my car. I knew the surprise in the letter was her way of ensuring I was provided for once more. I still haven't spent one dime of that money from her letter! I cherish it as I cherish her letter always.

Connecting through Clairsentience with My Grandparents

My grandparents weren't alive when Anthony and I got engaged on February 13, 2011. However, during one of the most significant times of our lives, I felt my grandparents the most. They made sure that—in some way from heaven—their participation in our wedding arrangements would help ease our stressful minds.

One of the first items on our to-do list was finding a hall. We wanted to make sure we found a close place for our guests. We had twelve places we wanted to visit. Midway on our search list was a wedding hall called the Riviera in Coney Island, Brooklyn. My husband had attended other weddings at this hall, and he already knew that he loved its theme. However, I hadn't been there at all.

As soon as I walked into the main dining area of the Riviera, I immediately felt Papa's intensity. I completely fell in love with the place. I was captivated by the golden-jeweled hue of cascading chandeliers, tables, chairs covered with crisp linen, and the soft-lighted sconces on the walls. The Riviera had been around for 120 years, and I absolutely admired its vintage décor. Most halls don't offer it anymore. Its salute to generations past equaled the vitality of Papa's presence I encountered that day. I detected him standing with me, approving the view, and appreciating the hospitality of the venue. I had prayed to my grandparents and my angels prior to visiting our many hall selections. I had asked them to surround us with people who had the best intentions for us with our wedding, which would enable us to connect with the right venue.

Everything I witnessed that day was proof that my prayers had been heard. I was completely sold on the Riviera, and I refused to look at another hall.

***

One of the highly anticipated parts of organizing a wedding is the bride-to-be's dress. I had subscribed to various wedding magazines and websites, and I dog-eared many images of could-be-the-one gowns in bridal books. Throughout my search in 2011, a particular designer, Mary's Bridal, captivated me. When it was finally time to venture out to the bridal stores, my parents and sister accompanied me.

The first store we visited did carry Mary's Bridal, but it was very far from my house. I decided to see if I could try some of the dresses there first and then find a store closer to me and order the dress that I decided on. The bridal consultant brought out a ginormous book to show me what she had in stock. When I was midway through the book, she showed me another selection. Unbeknownst to me, my mom's eyes lit up like a Christmas tree behind me—at the same time my curious eyes saw the dress. My mom secretly loved the dress and hoped I would stumble upon it.

The dressing room was slightly larger than a London phone booth, but I managed to fit the dress, the petticoat, the bridal consultant and myself inside. Since the dress didn't come in my size, I was clipped all around to fit into a larger one. There were no mirrors in the London phone booth. I would have to step outside and walk to a mirror. When the last clip was fastened, and before I was able to take those heart pounding steps toward the awaited view, a wave of invisible magic sparkled and swirled around me. The white on white—bridal ball gown from the Unspoken Romance Collection—sweetheart neckline, drop waist, lace applique cap sleeves, pearl, Swarovski, and bead embellishments, detachable royal length train, and zipper back with buttons—felt just my size.

Though the gown resembled Belle from *Beauty and the Beast*, I experienced my very own enchanting scene from *Cinderella*. I awaited my anxious reflection and emerged from the dressing room to see eager, hopeful eyes filled with blissful tears. My intuitive feelings stared right back at me, confirming that a fairy godmother had granted my wish.

In my case, the fairy godmother was my guardian angel—Grandma Marie. Prior to walking into the bridal shop that day, I had prayed to her ever so softly, to help me connect with "the one." The rest is history.

***

The day before my wedding, I gave myself some me time. It was a dazzling, laid-back Thursday afternoon in September. It still felt like summer—without the oppressive heat. Autumn was set to arrive in a few weeks. I was on my way home from the gym, which was a healthy twenty-five-minute walk, listening to various bands of choice on my MP3 Player. I was in a back and forth mix of being in the moment and not thinking, and then pondering what the next day would be like. With the gentlest breeze hugging my outer being and the afternoon sun playing tag with the trees around me, I unexpectedly had visitors. I felt and saw Grandma Marie and Papa walking with me. With their trusting arms around me, it resembled a Hallmark card or a Campbell's soup commercial.

I didn't specifically see the detailed features of my grandparents, but I felt and saw them as if I was walking behind us. I watched the affectionate scene with appreciation. I saw our detailed outlines mixed with warm hues of green, white, and yellow. I understood this tender moment, and without a single word, I received their blessings for my wedding, their promise to always be by my side, and their astonishment at how I'd grown up so fast. It was one of my favorite moments of contact with them.

***

During my early twenties, I moved downstairs to Papa and Grandma Rose's apartment so I could have more privacy. My sister would be able to have my old room. I stayed in my father's old room downstairs; he had lived on that floor before my parents were married. Whenever I was in my new room, especially if I was organizing my belongings, I would feel as if someone was watching me. It wasn't scary or creepy; it was a positive, accepting presence. I was drawn to this energy and smiled. I wholeheartedly knew it was Papa. I would sense him by the doorway. It was as if he didn't want to scare me by entering. He just wanted to watch from afar and see the changes I was making. I could tell he liked the progress of the room. With my mind's eye, I could see his arms behind his back and his nods of approval.

When he didn't approve of something, he made it known. Now that I'm older, I'm able to put the pattern together. Whenever I was getting ready to go out on a date, I would always feel a rushed moving energy/force behind me. It felt like someone was running up from behind me to get my attention. Imagine playing Red Light, Green Light, One, Two, Three and expecting, someone to tag you at any moment! That was the same urgent energy I felt. It would stop, start, and stop again at various times.

At first, it worried me a bit. I didn't expect it and had never encountered such an experience. I thought, *I'm imagining things. I'm just worrying myself since I'm downstairs alone at night.*

Despite the unknown, I didn't feel that any harm would come of it. I couldn't understand why I was receiving such a unique type of contact. The messages from your angels and those who have passed away will not derive from a negative source. The source of these messages are always pure and loving. People experiencing these intuitive moments for the first time may feel scared, but that is only because it is the unknown. Your angels and loved ones aren't trying to scare you.

As you learn the many communication styles of your loved ones, you can choose how to receive contact in a way that makes you feel comfortable. If you are more comfortable receiving messages through hearing, you can ask your angels or loved ones to connect with you that way. There is no need though to specify exactly what you want to hear; that will only limit what you are supposed to experience.

About two years later, the rushed feeling ceased—at the same time I started to date my future husband. I realized Papa was trying to warn me about whomever I was dating then. It all made sense when I was older. Papa probably felt that my safety or well-being was not melding with whomever I was with. Some of the relationships ended in friendships. Despite it all, I value every experience and relationship. They have made me appreciate what I wanted for my future—and I absolutely love and admire my husband today. Papa was trying to ensure that I saw the bigger picture in certain situations. I'm so thankful for that kind of guidance.

Connecting with my Grandparents through Clairaudience

On March 12, 2015, I was greeting clients near the reception desk at my office, when I noticed one of the guests had a butterfly necklace and a handbag with butterfly images all over. I was shocked when I saw this because in corporate settings, handbag accessories are usually solid colors—without any images. I found this quite refreshing and rather important. I instantly knew it was a sign from my grandparents. They were saying hello.

A wonderful woman works at my office, Mrs. C. She sets up the food and coffee for our meetings and maintains the kitchen. She is like the office mom/grandmother to us all. Mrs. C has so much stamina and pep in her soul; it's absolutely incredible for her age. On March 12, 2015, she started singing to me in Italian. This was the first time that I heard Mrs. C sing in Italian. Without batting an eyelash, I knew the butterfly messages leading up to her singing had been from Grandma Marie. Even though it was through two people, these outlets are also possible for receiving messages from your loved ones.

As I mentioned earlier in this book, my grandmother would always sing Italian, and butterflies were always something I would see regarding my grandparents connecting with me. I realized though, for all the above to happen on March 12 was more than just Grandma Marie saying hello. It was the fourth anniversary of Grandma Marie's passing. It was her way of confirming that she was healthy and in her restoration/growth stages. To receive that specific sign on that day was magnificent!

***

There is no need to wait for a dramatic or large-scale message or sign to make its presence known to you. Messages and signs can arrive in all shapes and sizes. The littlest everyday conveniences can be powerful. If you think of your grandparents while you are searching for a parking spot, you might suddenly find one. If you are waiting for a bus and hoping you didn't miss your scheduled one, your bus might approach. The list goes on and on.

CHAPTER VIII

Letters from Home—
Staying Connected

Death is nothing else but going home to God, the bond of love will be unbroken for all eternity.

—Mother Teresa

Grandparents never truly leave our side. We may not physically see them, but their memories, essences, and love still remain close. Faith brings their connection with us, to life. This reminds me of the 1960 TV film, that I adored watching as a child; *Peter Pan*, staring Mary Martin. In order for Tinkerbell to be well and fly, children around the world had to clap their hands long enough and believe in fairies. This would make Tinkerbell's light glow stronger. As you nurture your belief and your ability to connect with your grandparents, the stronger the frequency will be for them to enter your life, and your experiences with them will flourish endlessly.

I believe that when our loved ones pass, it isn't goodbye, rather, "until we meet again." I like to think of it as, they are away on a long trip, and when it's time to come home, we will reunite. This helps me get through the transitioning process and connect with my grandparents. You can also apply the following methods with anyone who has had an impact on your life.

The most familiar ways to keep the lines of communication open with your grandparents is through prayer and meditation. There is a difference between the two. Prayers involve speaking to God—or to whomever you feel most comfortable with—requesting assistance or guidance, asking for protection, or saying grace. Meditating is the art of going within yourself and clearing your mind of any cluttering thoughts. It is a time to be quiet and be within the moment; it is not a time for speaking.

Before practicing mediation, prayer, or any of the other examples in this chapter, try performing the following steps to enhance your connection with your grandparents:

❖ Center yourself. Go into meditation with the positive intention of communicating with your grandparents. What messages would you like to receive from them? Once you've established this, your mind should stay clear. No thinking—just being. If any thoughts pop up, let them fall to the side. Answers and messages will follow the meditation, but there is a possibility you might receive signs from your five senses during meditation. Pray to Archangel Michael, Archangel Raphael, or whomever you feel most comfortable with to protect and guide you through meditation. Envision white (purity), pink (love), green (healing), and purple (intuitive) light surrounding you. If you can't recall what colors to picture around you, think of a rainbow surrounding you.

❖ Sit upright in a comfortable chair in a quiet, relaxing room or setting.

❖ Safely light soothing, scented candles and play gentle music.

❖ Look at pictures of your grandparents or items that remind you of them.

❖ Close your eyes and remember a harmonious time you shared with your grandparents. Recall every detail and use all of your senses. Let go of any thoughts not related to your grandparents and focus on the present moment.

❖ Within your mind, tell your grandparents you love them and wish to connect with them.

❖ Visualize hugging your grandparents with the intent that you will see them again soon. Stay within this calming energy as long as you wish and until you're ready to end the meditation.

❖ Open your eyes, surrender, and release any concerns you have about receiving connection. You will encounter the messages according to divine timing.

Pen to Paper

One of my favorite ways to express my feelings is through writing. For me, this art is therapeutic, liberating, enchanting, humorous, quiet, indulging, supportive, and resourceful. Writing reveals worlds within you that you never knew existed. Once they are exposed, they feel familiar. It's a reminder of the voice within you.

Have you ever considered writing a book about your grandparents who have passed? It doesn't have to be published, but a book about your grandparents' lives can be passed down from generation to generation. It's like a scrapbook, but instead of pictures and stickers, you're displaying memories through words. It doesn't matter if you're not as skilled or crafty with your writing; all that counts is that it comes from the heart.

For me, writing this book has enhanced my connection with my grandparents tremendously. I was able to learn about their characters, revisit treasured remembrances, and heal parts of myself I didn't know needed healing. This method could work in a similar way for you if you're willing to dig deep. If you don't want to write a book, you can compose a diary of memories for yourself. Sharing your experiences with others can ignite a similar healing in them.

***

Journal writing is another way I stay connected with my grandparents. I have four journals—two for writing and two for organizing greeting cards. You can purchase decorative journals that match the personality of your grandparent. You can decorate your own or make one on Shutterfly.com.

In my journals, I talk to my grandparents by composing what my day was like, any exciting news regarding my family, advice needed, or any other day-to-day conversation. Setting a specific time to write to your grandparents will increase the connection. For example, I would to talk on the phone with Grandma Marie every Friday night at eight. I try to connect with Grandma Marie during that time through my journal writing.

Journal writing is private—between you and your grandparent—and you don't have to worry about grammar or spelling. It's all about freely expressing the true intentions of your heart; there is no pressure. My journal writing is very effective, especially when Grandma Marie responded to one of my journal entries with her last written letter before she passed away. My father finding that letter was not a coincidence. Everything happens for a reason—extraordinary ones indeed!

A greeting card journal is another favorite way I converse with my grandparents. You can purchase any type of journal that represents your bond with your grandparents. I was able to find one that I absolutely love, and it is organized by month. You can also rely on your imagination and design your own.

For holidays and birthdays, I purchase greeting cards for my grandparents. I write messages inside and organize them in the journal. I find cards that reflect our relationships while they were on earth. You'll know how to do this when you come across a card that stands out and lovingly tugs at your heart. For Halloween, Valentine's Day, or Easter, I channel their energy and choose cards that resemble childlike, cherished messages. For Mother's Day, Father's Day, and birthdays, I pick something that fits their personalities. For Christmas, I select cards with Jesus or other spiritual images and messages. I write thankful notes to Jesus, my angels, and my grandparents. I make it a point to let them all know how grateful I am for their constant guidance, love, and motivation. When I look through my journals, I think about all the different cards I've collected through the years. It always brings a smile to my being to see the uniqueness of each card and how my collection has progressed.

One journal I have has an inside flap where I collect various memorabilia. For Grandma Marie, I have photos, the last letter she wrote, *Wizard of Oz* items, and toothpicks. *(Whenever I went out to eat—whether Grandma was with me or not—I would grab toothpicks at the counter for her. I still collect them for her today.)* For Papa, I have pictures and a collection of red and white bakery string as keepsakes.

Poetry, songwriting, and playing instruments are other channels to explore. They can help release any pain you have and connect your energy with your grandparents. Arranging lines, lyrics, and music creatively can be a beacon of light to those who are trying to find a voice after a loss. Blogging is another way to reach people and connect with them instantly. This support system develops community and family for those who need it most.

Generation to Generation

Besides the beauty and creativity of connecting with words, you can also keep the line of communication flowing—and your grandparents' essence alive—by carrying down or sharing traditions and legacies with others. Connecting with your grandparents in the following ways listed, will open other channels of communication and provide other forms of necessary healing.

Cooking favorite meals that your grandparents once prepared is a great way to get everyone together to share a comforting time. Try to find old recipe books or call family members and trade recipe stories/secrets that you can make on your own. Cooking by yourself or with other family members enables you to reminisce about special stories close to your heart that are linked to various meals.

If you have children, you can share Grandma's famous baking recipes, which are always enjoyable to do together. My Mother-in-law Nina and I each year for Christmas make her mother's sugar cookies recipe along with my husband Anthony, my father-in-law Don, and my brother-in-laws John and Andrew. It's quite ironic that my mother-in-law dreads baking since it requires "sifting" through time and "kneading" of patience. She cringes at the sound of any baking term. To appease your courageous—inquisitive mind, just start off a conversation with *batter* or *cookie press*, and Nina will tell you how she "really feels" about baking. On a more serious note though, we all lighten her load with extra manpower in the kitchen. I'm certain that deep down, her knowing we are all together making something from her mom's past is gratifying.

In addition, Nina sometimes makes her mother's homemade crumb cake. I like the consistency and I'm intrigued by how the crumbs were made from scratch. Nina's mother's cookbook is filled with tons of recipes of her own and recipes she wanted to try. Get your hands on any cookbooks your grandparents left behind. You can learn a great deal about your family and your culture through every bite!

I absolutely couldn't get enough of Grandma Marie's potato and egg sandwiches. She would fry cubed potatoes in a pan with a little bit of oil. She cracked an egg over the potatoes, flipped it, and sprinkled Parmesan cheese on top. Served with soft rolls, it was always deliciously filling. She also made comforting soup that I now prepare quite often in the winter … lentil soup with elbow macaroni and Pecorino Romano cheese. I also cook a favorite dish of Papa's: rice with tomato sauce and ricotta. This combo may seem a bit out of the ordinary, but it's actually quite creamy and savory.

Sewing, quilting, crocheting, and needlepoint can be interesting. There is an endless stream of creations that you can make, including blankets, sweaters, scarves, hats, and booties. You can continue these projects from where your grandparents left off or create new ones. You can pass them down to your children. Mastering these techniques can provide hours of relaxation and will steady your mind for receiving messages from your grandparents.

Setting up foundations in your grandparents' names, joining leagues, and donating to clubs or organizations are generous ways to keep their memories alive. If your grandparent died from cancer or Alzheimer's, was a war vet, or was an advocate for helping children learn to read, you can raise money and promote awareness through foundations, leagues, clubs, and other organizations.

You can pass down family heirlooms: pocket watches, medals, garments, costume jewelry, wedding bands, furniture, tea sets, sports memorabilia, tapestries, family crests, letters from wars, flags, cars, or coin and stamp collections. Each piece contains history, emotions, culture, and answers. Some items can enrich the lives of others. Ancestry. com and Ellis Island are other places to explore your family's past.

Keep Them Close to Your Heart

If you stay connected with your loved ones, you can keep your mind active, your heart open, and your soul nurtured. You are not limited to the suggestions I mentioned. They are based on my experiences and serve as examples for you. You can generate ones with your own creative spark.

You may have started something that satisfies your needs, and that is absolutely wonderful! Make sure that whatever you choose resonates with your heart, comes from a positive source, and isn't rooted in addictions that only temporarily numb the pain.

Wearing a grandparent's birthstone or other jewelry can keep the memory of your loved one close. I purchased three angel necklaces; each held a heart that contained different color jewels at the center to represent the birthstones of my grandparents. Some people wear cremation jewelry: necklaces, lockets, crosses, charm bracelets, key chains, and other creatively embellished pendants.

I also purchased an angel figurine that channeled my grandparents' energy. The carved wood on the small figurine showcases a wavy, brown haired angel, a cream and silver dress, expansive wings, and a small butterfly over the palm of her hands. On the bottom of the angel's dress, the word *"serenity"* is painted in a brown swirly script. This message serves as a constant reminder from my grandparents that peace will always remain in my heart and soul—and nothing can take that away from me.

Keeping flowers of the birth month of your grandparents by your nightstand or planting a peaceful memorial garden in your backyard are excellent ways to tap into the therapeutic properties of nature. It can heighten your connection with your grandparents. There are so many elements you can add to your garden: angel statues, plaques with prayers and/or affirmations, plaques with pictures of your loved ones, pavers or stepping-stones, wicker benches, wind chimes, and fountains.

This is your safe haven; make it represent all that embodies the memory you wish to celebrate. You can even set up a memorial inside your home—on a mantel in your living room or study—if your loved one was cremated.

You can create a video montage for a special occasion to honor your loved ones. You can arrange a video or a slide show or display framed photos, photo albums, poems, candles, and other memorabilia. I've attended two weddings after getting married, and I was deeply moved by the displays for their grandparents.

Lastly, if you're open to the idea, you can also reach out to your grandparents through a certified medium. Mediums are able to connect with spirit and the energy of those who have passed away. These sessions deliver specific messages of closure, enlightenment, forgiveness and love between you and those who have left this earth. Through your visits with a medium, you can also confirm the wellness of those you love who are now in heaven. Mediumship is a safe, tranquil, harmonious and miraculous experience that can truly keep the line of communication flowing between you and your loved ones.

Even if time doesn't allow you to accomplish all that I have shared in this chapter, merely talking about your grandparents and sharing their stories and memories can keep your connection strong. Light a candle at the table during the holidays to remember those who couldn't physically be present. Lighting candles for birthdays also helps you stay in tune with your grandparents.

There is no specific way to celebrate the life of a departed soul or keep a connection with them. As long as your intentions are of the highest good—and you are patient during the transitioning period—you will constantly be amazed by how in tune you really are and how your grandparents and loved ones remain constant forces in your life.

CHAPTER IX

This Isn't Good-Bye!

There may be challenging days ahead. You might find it difficult to think about your grandparents, or other loved ones without crying or feeling lost. Some days may seem like the worst you've ever experienced, but other days will flow better than previous ones. This emotional roller-coaster ride may happen when the loss is still fresh or after much time has passed. This is all perfectly normal, and you shouldn't be ashamed or worried. I sometimes am in awe that Grandma Marie isn't physically on this earth, and it's been four years since she passed.

You can bounce back from these swirling sentiments as each day passes. Time heals wounds, but it does take time. It may not seem like there's any chance or hope that it will, but you will take little steps that you weren't able to do the day before. You have to be patient with yourself and progress with what feels right to you.

There is so much that encompasses you—and echoes the values of your grandparents. They are reaching out to you now to let you know they are just a thought away. If you have children, you may even see characteristics of your grandparents in them, which is truly a blessing to behold. This other level of connecting helps heal you; it is not a burden. When the day comes that my family grows, I will definitely be ecstatic to share my stories and recollections with my children. I will make them aware of all the precious attributes that flow within their veins. You can do the same with your children.

The ways your grandparents communicate with you may go beyond the scope of what I have mentioned here. I welcome this experience for you all and for myself. Maybe I can reconnect with you and share the new ways I've made contact with my grandparents. There is never a limit to what we can know and feel—as long as we are open to it. We are always evolving and adapting to new situations. If we say we have learned everything, then we have surely missed something!

I believe that my grandparents passed away at different times for a reason. Our missions on this earth were intertwined, and we needed to fulfill our own growth plans, which are based on how they affect our lives. The cover image for this book, which was created by the talented Joseph Bartolotta, captures this significance clearly. In his mind-blowing cover art, he knew where to place my grandparents without me telling him. The only bit of information that Joseph was aware of was what my grandparents looked like from the photos I showed him. He had no knowledge of my unique connection to each of them.

Joseph intuitively drew the angel looking into the reflecting pool as my father's mother-- Grandma Rose is watching Papa, Grandma Marie, and myself in the reflecting pool. Since Grandma Rose died before I was born, it was quite fitting to have her be the angel watching over me first from heaven. Her personality lives strongly within me.

Papa and Grandma Marie were with me at different stages of my life—during my childhood—Papa and Grandma Marie were with me during my adulthood. The three of us together in the reflecting pool is a culmination of our paths. I asked Joseph to add butterflies as symbols of my grandparents' constant vigilance and the inspiring transformation of life. I was completely speechless by the visual magnificence Joseph created and captured with the mediums he used. I believe my grandparents joined him in revealing the expression of their stories. I'm forever appreciative of what Joseph was able to accomplish through his innate ability.

This isn't it! This isn't good-bye! I believe with all my heart that you will see your grandparents again. When it's time to go home, you will recognize each other's souls and remember the connections you once shared on earth—and in many other lifetimes. Don't give up on this! You have much left to fulfill in your mission here on earth—even though your grandparents have finished their missions for now. The place they currently reside will enable them to help you more than they could before. Constantly pray for their guidance—as well as to your angels. You are worthy of receiving their blessed messages.

I close with a saying that in its simplicity provides, guidance, inspiration, and comfort to the faithful. May serenity always find its way to your heart and soul.

> *Those we love don't go away, they walk beside us every day. Unseen, unheard but always near, still loved, still missed and very dear. Love leaves a memory no one can steal.*

—Author unknown

RESOURCES

James Van Praagh. *Adventures of the Soul: Journeys through the Physical and Spiritual Dimensions.* Hay House, 2014.

NYCHA Housing Developments. "Alfred E. Smith Houses." Accessed April 22, 2015. http://www.nyc.gov/html/nycha/html/devopments/mansmith.shtml.

NYC in Focus. Accessed April 22, 2015. http://nycinfocus.org/where-we-are/alfred-e-smith-houses/.

Ancestry. http://www.ancestry.com.

Doreen Virtue. *Archangels and Ascended Masters: A Guide to Working and Healing with Divinities and Deities.* Hay House, 2004.

Esther Hicks and Jerry Hicks. *The Amazing Power of Deliberate Intent. Living the Art of Allowing.* Hay House, 2007.

The Auras Expert. "Auras." http://www.the-auras-expert.com/aura-colors-meaning.html. Copyright: 2006–2015.

IMBD. *"Awakenings* Movie Quotes." http://www.imdb.com/title/tt0099077/quotes. Copyright 1990–2015.

End Quote of Book from Board of Wisdom. http://boardofwisdom.com/togo/Quotes/ShowQuote/?msgid=282227, 2014

Doreen Virtue. *Chakra Clearing: Awakening Your Spiritual Power to Know and Heal.* Hay House, 1998.

Think Exist. "Eskimo Proverb." http://thinkexist.com/quotation/perhaps_they_are_not_stars-but_rather_openings_in/254756.html, Copyright 1999–2015.

Terri Guillemets. The Quote Garden. "Grandparent Quotes from Authors Unknown and Marcy Demaree." Originally self-published 1998. http://www.quotegarden.com.

Wikipedia: The Free Encyclopedia. Wikimedia Foundation, Inc. "Great Depression." Accessed March, 31, 2015. http://en.wikipedia.org/wiki/Great_Depression.

Good Reads. "Helen Keller Quotes." http://www.goodreads.com/author/quotes/7275.Helen_Keller.

Doreen Virtue and James Van Praagh. *How to Heal a Grieving Heart.* Hay House, 2014.

Man in the Red Bandanna. http://espn.go.com/video/clip?id=11505494, 2014.

Jonathan Lockwood Huie Inspirational Quotes about Life. "Mother Teresa Quotes." http://www.quotes-inspirational.com/quote/death-nothing-else-going-home-112/.

AZ Lyrics. "Over The Rainbow." http://www.azlyrics.com/lyrics/judygarland/overtherainbow.html, Copyright 20102015.

Gertrude Tooley Buckingham. *Poems at Random.* Kimball Press, 1948.

James Vann Praagh. *Talking to Heaven: A Mediumship's Message of Life after Death.* Penguin Publishing Group, 2001.

Doreen Virtue and James Van Praagh. *Talking to Heaven Mediumship Cards.* Hay House, 2013.

Wikipedia: The Free Encyclopedia. Wikimedia Foundation, Inc. "WWII." Accessed March 10, 2015. http://en.wikipeida.org/wiki/World_War_II.

About the Author

Andrea R. Freeman is a Certified Angel Card Reader and Angelic Life Coach with clairvoyant and clairsentient intuitive abilities. Andrea's spiritual knowledge includes metaphysical and Reiki studies. Connecting her clients with their guardian angels' loving messages is an uplifting experience that Andrea truly enjoys witnessing time and time again. Knowing that she is contributing toward others awakening to their life purposes is beyond fulfilling. When she first conducted readings for herself, she discovered that the comforting wisdom she received would inspire others and reveal what life truly can offer.

Andrea conducts one-on-one readings in person in New York and Ocean City, Maryland. She also gives readings via phone and e-mail for other areas outside New York. Her blog, Aerobic Affirmations, develops positive intentions geared toward your daily thoughts on life. She demonstrates that when your thoughts are more grounded, focused, and optimistic, you're better able to attract all the good that is waiting to align with you. You can find Andrea's blog at: aerobicaffirmations. blogspot.com.

Messages from My Grandparents is Andrea's first book, and she has other books currently in the works of different genres. Her other featured writings include an online food and wine piece with the former Yahoo Voices called "Turkish Cuisine by the Beach." It can now be found on her blog: gobblersvoyage.travellerspoint.com. Andrea's other blogs are twoweeks.travellerspoint.com and icecreamandcroutons.blogspot.com.

To stay up-to-date with Andrea, you can follow her via:

- ❖ Facebook: AngelicMotivation333
- ❖ Twitter: @AngelicReading
- ❖ Instagram: AngelicMotivation
- ❖ Website: www.angelicmotivation.com

ABOUT THE ARTIST

Joseph Bartolotta is a New York–based illustrator. He studied at the Fashion Institute of Technology, but he has been sketching out the fantastic worlds and characters of his overactive imagination since he could hold a pencil. From the time he was three, he could be found quietly drawing his daydreams for hours on end. In addition to the cover art for this book, Joseph illustrated his first children's book in 2015 (*Aunt Noodle and Her Friends* by Diane Marie Riendeau). He is also a freelance portrait artist and muralist.

The cover art and illustrations for Andrea's *Messages from My Grandparents* were created with mixed media. Working in layers of fixative, pencil, ink, colored pencil, and watercolors, Joseph found great inspiration in the subject matter. He identifies as a sensitive (mainly an empath with some clairaudience, clairsentience, and clairvoyance). Although always sensitive, as a challenged teen he dabbled in the occult in a search for God and identity. Ultimately, the intervention of angels brought him safely out of some dark wanderings and back into a loving relationship with God. Despite his efforts to deny them and tune them out for fear of reengaging darker associations, Joseph continued to retain his sensitivity to these unseen forces.

Joseph's meeting and collaborating with Andrea was serendipitous. It marked the start of getting back on track with his given path, conquering fear, embracing his gifts, and empowering his callings as an individual and as an artist.

Joseph is mainly an actor by trade. You may view his work at www. josephbartolotta.tv. A link to his visual art will be added there soon.

Printed in the United States
By Bookmasters